Sheridan
Interviews and Recollections

SHERIDAN

Interviews and Recollections

Edited by

E. H. Mikhail
Professor of English
University of Lethbridge, Alberta

St. Martin's Press   New York

Selection and editorial matter © E. H. Mikhail 1989

All rights reserved. For information write:
Scholarly and Reference Division,
St. Martin's Press, Inc., 175 Fifth Avenue, New York, NY 10010

First published in the United States of America in 1989

Printed in the People's Republic of China

ISBN 0-312-03013-4

Library of Congress Cataloging-in-Publication Data
Sheridan: interviews and recollections.

   Bibliography: p.
   Includes index.
   1. Sheridan, Richard Brinsley, 1751–1816—Biography.
2. Dramatists, English—18th century—Biography.
3. Theatrical managers—Great Britain—Biography.
4. Legislators—Great Britain—Biography.
I. Mikhail, E. H.
PR3683.S595   1989   822'.6   [B]   88-35562
ISBN 0-312-03013-4

Contents

Acknowledgements vii

Introduction ix

A Note on the Text xv

Chronological Table xvi

INTERVIEWS AND RECOLLECTIONS

Early Days	*Alicia Sheridan*	1
Harlequin Schoolboy	*Samuel Parr*	2
Sheridan at Harrow	*Alicia Lefanu*	5
The Elopement	*Elizabeth Sheridan*	7
Announcement	*Thomas Mathews*	10
Tormenting Expectation	*Richard Brinsley Sheridan*	11
A Duel	*Richard Brinsley Sheridan*	12
Proper Satisfaction	*Charles Francis Sheridan*	13
A Second Duel	*Bath Chronicle*	15
Deepest Concern	*Charles Francis Sheridan*	16
Wonderfully Recovered	*Thomas Sheridan*	17
No, by God, I Won't	*William Barnett*	19
Playful Talent	*Henry Angelo*	21
The Rivals	*Mary Linley*	23
The Duenna	*Thomas Linley*	24
The School for Scandal	*Frederic Reynolds*	25
By My Own Son	*Thomas Sheridan*	26
Sheridan and Cumberland	*Stanley Thomas Williams*	27
Extremely Happy	*Fanny Burney*	36
At Drury Lane	*Mrs Siddons*	37
Meets Fox	*Lord John Townshend*	38
In Parliament	*Sir Nathaniel Wraxall*	39
The Orator	*Sir Gilbert Elliot*	40
Witchcraft	*Sir Horace Walpole*	41
Pride Filled My Heart	*Elizabeth Sheridan* [Sheridan's sister]	42
Dick's Triumph	*Elizabeth Sheridan* [Sheridan's wife]	43
Tumult of Applause		44

Done with the Stage	Charles Dibdin	45
By His Father's Side	Dr Daniel Jarvis	46
My Brother's Kindness	Elizabeth Sheridan [Sheridan's sister]	48
The Excessive Drinker	Elizabeth Sheridan [Sheridan's wife]	49
My Dearest Hetty	Elizabeth Sheridan [Sheridan's wife]	50
Fading in Sickness	Richard Brinsley Sheridan	54
An Agonising Scene	Mrs Stratford Canning	55
Tom's Tutor	William Smyth	57
The Angel is Dying	Mrs Stratford Canning	62
Pecuniary Matters	William Smyth	63
A Ludicrous Line	Samuel Taylor Coleridge	65
Sheridan Called	Lady Bessborough	66
Sheridan Called Again	Lady Bessborough	67
Recollections of Sheridan	John Philip Kemble	69
Recollections of Sheridan	Elizabeth Lady Holland	73
Never Sober	Lady Bessborough	78
Dick's Astonishment	Charles Francis Sheridan	79
I Thought I Knew Brinsley	Charles Francis Sheridan	80
A Difficult Position	Thomas Creevey	81
A Distressing Evening	Anne Mathews	82
Recollections of Sheridan	Michael Kelly	83
Mr Sheridan	Lord Henry Brougham	92
Recollections of Sheridan	Lord Byron	96
A Dying Man	George IV	97
Remember Me		105
Sheridan's Funeral	Lord Broughton	106
A Great Man	George IV	107
Recollections of Sheridan	Samuel Rogers	108
He Beats Them All	Lord Byron	111
More Recollections of Sheridan	Lord Byron	112
In Defence of Sheridan	Alicia Lefanu	114
Mr Sheridan	Charles Butler	128
The Character of Sheridan	William Cullen Bryant	134
The Real Sheridan	The Marquis of Dufferin and Ava	137

Bibliography   139

Index   147

Acknowledgements

My gratitude is due to the following for assistance, support, encouragement, information, editorial material, or notification of certain items that appear in this book: Professor William A. Armstrong, Mr Edwin Ellis, Mr John Fitzgerald, Miss Joanne Grant, Dr M. Gudrun Hesse, Miss Rosemary Howard, Dr William Latta, Jr, Dr Christopher Murray, Mrs Lorna Newman, Dr Brent D. Shaw, Miss Sharon Walker, and Mrs Linda Wood.

The book has benefited greatly from comments and suggestions made by Dr Richard Arnold.

I am greatly indebted to Mrs Charlene Sawatsky and Miss Bea Ramtej for their kindness and patience in the final preparation of the typescript.

Several publications have been of immense help to me, particularly Jack D. Durant, *Richard Brinsley Sheridan: A Reference Guide* (Boston, Mass.: G. K. Hall, 1981).

It is also a pleasant duty to record my appreciation of the staff of the University of Lethbridge Library; the National Library of Canada, Ottawa; the National Library of Ireland, Dublin; Trinity College Library, Dublin; the British Library, London; the Newspaper Library, Colindale; and the New York Public Library.

Introduction

'The real Sheridan, as he was in private life, is irrevocably gone', said the *Encyclopaedia Britannica* of 1886. Sheridan's character is so full of contradictions that it is difficult to assess. His biographers have been painstaking but hardly penetrating. Thomas Moore, in his posthumous *Journals*, let us into the secret of his frustration. He says, 'I am quite sick of this life of Sheridan. I can learn nothing about him. I am going to call on Sukey Ogle to ascertain if she can tell me anything.' Contradiction runs through Sheridan's whole life. He was a poor man who was concerned with large sums of money. He won the heart of Elizabeth Linley by his delicacy, and wounded it cruelly by his infidelity. He was a friend to the national economy, though the course of his own life was never regulated on that principle. But the most remarkable aspect of his nature was his faculty for making others act in a manner contrary to their wishes, for getting his own way against apparently insuperable odds, coupled with a miraculous inability to offend people. 'Everybody in the world speaks well of him', says Sir Peter Teazle in *The School for Scandal*. 'I am sorry to hear it,' replies Sir Oliver Surface, 'he has too good a character to be an honest fellow. Everybody speaks well of him! Psha! then he has bowed as low to knaves and fools as to the honest dignity of genius and virtue.' Everybody did not speak well of Sheridan; he owed too much money and was a little too honest for that; but he was quite incapable of arousing hostility. 'He *could not* make enemies', wrote Hazlitt. 'If anyone came to request the repayment of a loan from him, he borrowed more. A cordial shake of his hand was a receipt in full for all demands. He could 'coin his *smile* for drachmas', cancel bonds with *bon mots*, and give jokes in discharge of a bill. A friend of his said, 'If I pull off my hat to him in the street, it costs me fifty pounds, and if he speaks to me it's a hundred!' There was something elusive about Sheridan – something almost secretive. He loved to make a mystery of his doings. He is often mentioned in the memoirs and diaries of the time, but he himself kept no diary and wrote no memoirs – a fact which would not have surprised anyone who knew him. It was a letter-writing age, but he had no love for writing letters, and those written to him lay only too often and too long unopened on his table or in his letter-bag.

Sheridan made so great a reputation as a playwright and conversational wit that his company was the delight alike of London drawing-rooms, country houses, clubs, coffee houses, and taverns. Of Sheridan in company and as a talker some accounts have been given. His talk beguiled Georgiana, Duchess of Devonshire, to stay at Chatsworth two months beyond her intention while the expenses of the house she had taken at Bath piled themselves up unregarded. If he was watching a performance at Drury Lane or elsewhere, no thought of retiring home would enter his mind when the curtain came down in the final act. There was always Brooks's to go to; or the Beefsteak Club, where he might meet Charles Fox, whom of all other men Sheridan delighted to amaze, 'firing and blazing away for the evening, like an inexhaustible battery',[1] as on that memorable evening described by John Bernard when 'Fox was seated between Sheridan and Bannister, and did nothing but fill their glasses and listen to their conversation; whilst they, making head a kind of shuttlecock, hit it on each side with such admirable repartees, that he roared aloud like a bull.'[2] Sheridan had become acquainted with Fox by means of Lord John Townshend. 'I made the first dinner party', says his Lordship,

> at which they met; having told Fox that all the notions he might have conceived of Sheridan's talents and genius, from the comedy of *The Rivals*, &c. would fall infinitely short of the admiration of his astonishing powers, which I was sure he would entertain at the first interview. The first interview between them (there were very few present, only Tickell and myself, and one or two more) I shall never forget; Fox told me, after breaking up from dinner, that he had always thought Hare, after my uncle Charles Townshend, the wittiest man he had ever met with, but that Sheridan surpassed them both infinitely.

Lord Byron, who knew Sheridan well, speaks of his conversation in eulogistic terms:

> In society I have met Sheridan frequently: he was superb. He had a sort of liking for me, and never attacked me, at least to my face, and he did everybody else – high names, and wits, and orators, some of them poets also. I have seen him cut Whitbread, quiz Madame de Staël, annihilate Colman, and do little less by some others (whose name, as friends, I set not down) of good fame and ability. I have met him in all places and parties – at Whitehall with the Melbournes, at the Marquis of Tavistock's, at Robins's the auctioneer's, at Sir Humphrey Davy's, at Sam Rogers's – in short, in most kinds of company, and always found him very convivial and delightful.

Lady Elizabeth Holland confided to her journal that, though she knew very well that Sheridan ought to be despised for his private life and suspected for his political conduct, her impulse was too much for her, and whenever she saw him, even if only for a few minutes, all these reasonable prejudices were at once put to flight. Lord Henry Holland found it impossible to be angry with Sheridan though he had just used in a speech the very information his Lordship meant to use himself and had imparted to Sheridan under a promise that he would not divulge it. Boswell sets down a conversation at the Literary Club when Sheridan was there, but, evidently repressed by the presence of his elders, he seems to have chosen not to immortalise it. Fanny Burney met him at Mrs Cholmondeley's, in 1779, and recorded her impressions at some length. William Windham noted in his diary that he met Sheridan at Mrs Crewe's in 1794, after the split in the Whig Party. 'The charm of his conversation', he wrote, 'and the memory of past times made me regret the differences that now separate us.' Michael Kelly remarked that Sheridan was a 'delightful companion'. Sheridan's charm was not due to vivacity, or to a flow of brilliant conversation. His good things were said only at intervals and where they came in naturally. He was silent as a rule, except when he saw a chance of saying something that was worth saying, and then he made his effect with unerring certainty. So brilliant indeed were his interpositions in conversation that people used to hint that they had been prepared beforehand, and that the attack was only delivered after a long course of elaborate manoeuvres. It may have been so in some cases, but certainly not in all, though we have little means of judging.

Sheridan had not one career, but three: he was a dramatist, the manager of a theatre, and a politician. The three careers, however, are not unrelated. If Sheridan had not written plays he would not have become the manager of Drury Lane, and if he had not been the manager of Drury Lane he would, in all probability, never have been able to enter Parliament. Sheridan is remembered for the brilliance of his comedies, which after more than two hundred years still have the magic to keep the audience laughing. Yet, of the forty years and upwards over which his career stretched, he gave no more than five to the writing of his plays. *The Rivals* came out in January 1775 and *The Critic* in October 1779. Between these two dates lies all that matters of Sheridan's career as a dramatist. His political career, on the other hand, lasted thirty-two years, which shows that nearly all his efforts and certainly most of his ambitions lay in the field of politics and the social activities which went with the politics of his era. Having reached, at twenty-six, the crowning point of his fame as a dramatic writer, Sheridan determined to try his luck in the world of practical politics. It is easy, therefore, to overlook the fact that the author of *The School for Scandal* was also a politician and an orator, but this is not, after all, very surprising, for his political career, though interesting, was not of outstanding importance; and when we think of Fox and Pitt we rarely remember that Sheridan was a distinguished follower of the former and a bitter and redoubtable enemy of the latter. Moreover, the fame of an orator soon wears thin. Had Sheridan but reserved his 'elegances' for the real stage, had he but known that the House of Commons was in very truth not 'the proper scene' for his gifts, posterity would have gained inestimably, and the orator might have had a much happier and more interesting life. Why did he, then, relegate his true talent – playwriting – to a secondary position in his life? The answers lie largely in what he himself saw of the theatre and theatrical life, in what he heard of it from his actor father, and in the struggle for gentility which was endemic in the family. In order to understand Sheridan's career, it is necessary always to keep in mind that he had only one deep ambition, and that this had nothing to do specifically either with the theatre or with politics. His determination was from the first to be an important figure in the little Great World of London Society. In the eighteenth century this was not the ignoble aspiration which it would appear today. It is almost true to say that if a man desired to live the perfect life in those days, he had to be both well-born and rich. Late-night socialising and 'clubbable' behaviour in the wee small hours were not unusual for the London wit-about-town, and for the innumerable would-be wits-about-town. When Sheridan died, it was universally agreed that the only fitting place of burial was Westminster Abbey, but, although he himself had desired to rest there near Fox, the authorities decided that the Poets' Corner, beside Garrick, was the appropriate spot. The choice was a tacit criticism, and acceptance of where his true genius lay.

It would indeed be hard to recall anyone so unfortunate as Sheridan in his biographers; nor would it be easy to find a more dissatisfied set of critics than those authors on the subject of each other's attempts. The chief difficulty which the biographer of Sheridan had to encounter was the task, not so much of discovering the truth about him, as of cutting it free from the monstrous entanglements of misunderstandings, prejudices, and flat falsehoods with which it is overgrown. Sheridan had no Boswell, and not even a Lockhart or a Forster. John Watkins,[3] who wrote the first life of Sheridan, had little personal knowledge of him, and Watkins' work, though published as early as 1817, has little value. Watkins was a political opponent and detractor and his *Memoirs* has fallen into oblivion. Thomas Moore,[4] at the request of Sheridan's second wife, wrote what may be called the official biography, founded upon the fullest information, with the help of all that Sheridan had left behind in the way of papers, and all that the family could furnish –

along with Moore's own personal recollections. However, it is not a very characteristic piece of work and greatly dissatisfied the friends and lovers of Sheridan. Moore was never on intimate terms with Sheridan, and did not meet him until after 1800. Besides, he was sometimes misinformed and ungenerous, and was too much in awe of the great personages of whom he had to write to do justice to his friend's political career. With the professed intention of making up for the absence of character in Moore's *Memoirs*, a small volume of *Sheridaniana*[5] was published the year after, which is full of amusing anecdotes, but little, if any, additional information. William Smyth, who was tutor to Sheridan's son Tom between 1792 and 1796, acceded to a request of Miss Cotton when he became Professor at Oxford and wrote his *Memoir*[6] of Sheridan. Smyth's brief sketch concerns only the latter part of Sheridan's life, but it is usually creditable as to fact, and is the most lifelife and, in many respects, the most touching contemporary portrait that has been made of Sheridan. Scarcely an edition of Sheridan's plays has been published (and they are numberless) without a biographical notice. The most noted of these is perhaps the 'Biographical and Critical Sketch'[7] of Leigh Hunt, which does not, however, pretend to any new light, and is entirely unsympathetic. Hunt undertakes to explain the waste of Sheridan's gifts, remarking his early habits of delay, his high animated spirits, and his love of luxury. William Earle, the 'Octogenarian',[8] promised to afford new information and to correct earlier biographies; but his work, except for certain dubious and not very savoury stories of the Prince Regent period, failed to do so. Mrs Oliphant[9] was approached by the editor of the English Men of Letters series, and in her biography of Sheridan she rises in all the outraged virtue of a Victorian matron confronted with Sin. Sheridan's next biography, provided by Percy Fitzgerald,[10] is full of inaccuracies. Lloyd Sanders,[11] like Mrs Oliphant, was approached by the editor of a literary series. In his biography he acknowledges that Sheridan the man was certainly a riddle. Sanders' biography was followed by that of W. Fraser Rae,[12] who wrote at the instance of a great-grandson of Sheridan. Although Rae undertook the task of writing a full and unprejudiced account, he omitted much and is sometimes monotonously laudatory. Thirteen years after Rae came Walter Sichel,[13] who published important new material which threw a great deal of fresh light on the subject.[14]

The present volume is a composite biography which provides a forum to most of those who were associated with Sheridan. The exigencies of space, however, limit the number of writers who can be included. I have aimed mostly at selecting those recollections that have not been reprinted, as well as those that are not readily available. The pieces, arranged in chronological order, cover almost all the stages of

Sheridan's life, so as to present as many facets as possible. It is hoped that the method used in this book will give a different impression from that of previous biographies, and, on balance, probably a truer one.

NOTES

1. John Bernard, *Retrospections of the Stage* (London, 1930) II, 142.
2. Ibid., p. 144.
3. John Watkins, *Memoirs of the Public and Private Life of the Right Honourable Richard Brinsley Sheridan, with a Particular Account of His Family and Connexions*, 2 vols (London: Henry Colburn, 1817).
4. Thomas Moore, *Memoirs of the Life of the Right Honourable Richard Brinsley Sheridan* (London: Longman, Hurst, Rees, Orme, Brown and Green, 1825).
5. *Sheridaniana; or Anecdotes of the Life of Richard Brinsley Sheridan, His Table Talk and Bon Mots* (London: Henry Colburn, 1826).
6. William Smyth, *Memoir of Mr Sheridan* (Leeds: J. Cross, 1840).
7. Leigh Hunt, 'Biographical and Critical Sketch', in Hunt (ed.), *The Dramatic Works of Richard Brinsley Sheridan* (London: Edward Moxon, 1840).
8. [William Earle,] *Sheridan and His Times by an Octogenarian, who Stood by His Knee in Youth and Sat at His Table in Manhood*, 2 vols (London: J. F. Hope, 1859).
9. Margaret Oliphant, *Sheridan*, English Men of Letters series (London: Macmillan, 1883).
10. Percy Fitzgerald, *The Lives of the Sheridans*, 2 vols (London: R. Bentley and Son, 1886).
11. Lloyd C. Sanders, *Life of Richard Brinsley Sheridan*, Great Writers series (London: Walter Scott, 1890).
12. W. Fraser Rae, *Sheridan: A Biography*, 2 vols (London: Richard Bentley, 1896).
13. Walter Sichel, *Sheridan, from New and Original Material; Including a Manuscript Diary by Georgiana, Duchess of Devonshire*, 2 vols (London: Constable, 1909).
14. Subsequent biographies of Sheridan are usually reliable. For details of these see Jack D. Durant, *Richard Brinsley Sheridan: A Reference Guide* (Boston, Mass.: G. K. Hall, 1981).

A Note on the Text

In the extracts given, typographical errors have been silently corrected, and the spelling of names has been rendered consistent throughout; otherwise, spelling has not been modernised or standardised. All titles of plays and books are in italics. Punctuation has not been altered, except that quotation marks are now always single in the first instance and placed in accordance with modern British convention, and contractions such as 'Mr' are not followed by a full point.

Chronological Table

1751	30 Oct: Richard Brinsley Sheridan born at 12 Dorset Street, Dublin. (His elder brother, Charles Francis, was born in 1750, and two sisters follow, Alicia in 1753 and Elizabeth in 1758). 4 Nov: Christened.
1757	Richard Brinsley attends Samuel Whyte's grammar school in Dublin.
1760	The Sheridan family moves to London, never to return to Dublin.
1762–8	Richard Brinsley attends Harrow School.
1764	Thomas Sheridan's financial problems continue to dog him and he decides to go with his family to live in France. Richard Brinsley is put under the care of his uncle Richard Chamberlaine, a London surgeon.
1766	22 Sep: Frances Anne Sheridan (mother) dies at Blois, in central France.
1770	The Sheridan family moves to Bath.
1771	Aug: *The Love Epistles of Aristaenetus*, a translation or free paraphrase from the Greek, appears.
1772	18 Mar: Elopes with Elizabeth Linley to France. 9 Apr: Thomas Mathews, Elizabeth's admirer, publishes in the *Bath Chronicle* what amounts to a challenge to Sheridan, posting him as a liar and a treacherous scoundrel. 4 May: Fights first duel with Thomas Mathews. 1 July: Fights second duel with Thomas Mathews. 27 Aug: Goes to Waltham Abbey in Essex to study law.
1773	6 Apr: Enters himself as a barrister in the Middle Temple. 13 Apr: Marries Elizabeth Ann Linley at Marylebone Church, London. Lives in a cottage at Burnham Grove.
1774	Spring: Moves to a house in Orchard Street, London. Nov: Writes to his father-in-law that he has been very seriously at work on a book.
1775	17 Jan: *The Rivals* produced at Covent Garden Theatre, and withdrawn immediately after the first night for alterations. 28 Jan: Revised version of *The Rivals* produced at Covent Garden Theatre.

	2 May: *St Patrick's Day* produced at Covent Garden Theatre. 17 Nov: Thomas Sheridan (first son) born. 21 Nov: *The Duenna* produced at Covent Garden Theatre.
1776	10 June: Garrick retires from the stage. 24 June: Sheridan signs the agreement which makes over Garrick's half of Drury Lane to himself and two partners. 21 Sep: Drury Lane Theatre opens for the new season under Sheridan's management.
1777	24 Feb: *A Trip to Scarborough* produced at Drury Lane Theatre. 14 Mar: Elected a member of Dr Samuel Johnson's exclusive Literary Club. 8 May: *The School for Scandal* produced at Drury Lane Theatre.
1778	Acquires remaining half-share in Drury Lane. 15 Nov: *The Camp* produced at Drury Lane Theatre.
1779	30 Oct: *The Critic* produced at Drury Lane Theatre.
1780	2 Feb: Makes first appearance in the character of a politician at Westminster Hall, in support of Charles Fox. 12 Sep: The second phase of Sheridan's career begins when he is elected to Parliament as the Member for Stafford. (He serves in Parliament until 1812). 23 Sep: Makes first speech in Parliament. 2 Nov: Elected to Brooks's Club, the Whig enclave recently built in St James's.
1781	21 Jan: *Robinson Crusoe* [a pantomime] produced at Drury Lane Theatre.
1782	Mar: Becomes Under-Secretary of State in Lord Rockingham's Cabinet.
1783	2 Apr: Becomes Secretary of Treasury in the Coalition Government under Lord North and Fox.
1787	7 Feb: Advances the charge against Warren Hastings in the House of Commons.
1788	13 Feb: The trial of Warren Hastings begins. Sheridan makes first speech against Hastings in Westminster Hall. 13 June: Makes last speech at trial of Hastings. (Previous speeches on 3, 6 and 10 June.) 14 Aug: Thomas Sheridan (father) dies.
1789	Sir Joshua Reynolds paints a portrait of Sheridan. The Bastille falls. Fox and Sheridan side with the French Revolution.
1790	Splits with Edmund Burke over the issue of the French Revolution.
1791	4 June: The last performance in Drury Lane Theatre given, the building having been condemned.

1792	30 Mar: Mary Sheridan (Elizabeth's baby by Lord Edward Fitzgerald?) born.
	28 June: Elizabeth Sheridan (wife) dies.
1793	23 Oct: Mary Sheridan dies.
1794	12 Mar: The new Drury Lane Theatre opens 'for the presentation of dramas'.
	14 May: Called on to reply on the Begums charge.
1795	27 Apr: marries Hester Jane Ogle, daughter of Newton Ogle, Dean of Winchester.
1796	14 Jan: Charles Brinsley Sheridan (second son) born.
1799	24 May: *Pizarro* produced.
1802	For the last time returned by the free and independent burgesses of Stafford.
1804	The Prince of Wales offers Sheridan the receivership of the Duchy of Cornwall. (Unfortunately, it soon appears that the place has already been promised to General, afterwards Lord, Lake.)
1806	Becomes Treasurer of Navy in 'All the Talents'.
	Fox dies. Sheridan succeeds Fox as Member for Westminster. Surrenders the directorship of his theatre to his son Tom.
	Charles Francis (brother) dies.
1807	Defeated at Westminster. Becomes Member for Ilchester.
1809	24 Feb: New Drury Lane Theatre burns down.
1811	Becomes Prince of Wales's chief adviser.
1812	21 July: Speaks in Parliament in support of the war with France: the House is never to hear him again.
	Oct: Defeated for Parliament.
	Loses Prince's favour.
	The rebuilt Drury Lane Theatre opens.
1813	Aug: Imprisoned for debt.
1814	May: Arrested for debt. (It is possible that he was arrested for debt on three other occasions: in August 1813, March 1814 and August 1815.)
1816	7 July: Dies at 17 Savile Row.
	13 July: Buried in Westminster Abbey.
1817	12 Sep: Tom Sheridan (son) dies.
	27 Oct: Hester Sheridan (second wife) dies.
1843	29 Nov: Charles Sheridan (son) dies.

Early Days*

ALICIA SHERIDAN

Of his childhood I have a very faint recollection; neither he nor I were very happy, but we were fondly attached to each other. We had no one else to love. My father's affections were fixed on his eldest son[1] and on my sister.[2] Had my mother lived our fate would have been different, for she had a spirit of justice that would have prevented her from showing favour towards any of her children but as they might deserve it. My brother at the age of ten years was sent to Harrow School[3] under the care of Dr Sumner who was a particular friend of my father's. For three years we never saw him except during the Christmas and summer vacation, periods that I looked forward to as the only happy hours my childhood was to know. We then were separated for four years which were spent, by my eldest brother, my sister and myself, in France. . . .[4]

At the end of two years we returned to England when I may say I became acquainted with my brother, for faint and imperfect were my recollections of him as might be expected from my age. I saw him, and my childish attachment revived with double force. He was handsome, not merely in the eyes of a partial sister but generally allowed to be so. His cheeks had the glow of health, his eyes, the finest in the world, the brilliancy of genius as soft and tender as an affectionate heart could render them, the same playful fancy, the same sterling and innoxious wit that was shown afterwards in his writings, cheered and delighted the family circle. I admired, I almost adored him, I would most willingly have sacrificed my life for him, as I in some measure proved to him at Bath where we resided for some time[5] and where events that you must have heard of engaged him in a duel.[6] My father's displeasure threatened to involve me in the denunciations against him for committing what he considered as a crime, yet I risked everything and eventually was made happy by obtaining forgiveness for my brother.

* From W. Fraser Rae, *Sheridan: A Biography* (London: Richard Bentley, 1896) i, 73–5.

NOTES

Alicia Sheridan (1753–1817), the elder of Sheridan's two sisters, was but two years younger than Sheridan and they were playmates; they suffered at the same time from children's ailments. When their parents quitted Dublin for London in 1760, they were left in charge of a nurse and they both received some instruction from Samuel Whyte at his grammar school in Dublin. Sheridan never revisited his native land. Alicia returned to it in 1773, became the second wife of Joseph Lefanu in 1781, and lived there till her death. This account of Sheridan's childhood was written on 9 November 1816 in the form of a letter to Sheridan's widow, four months after his death, in reply to a request for particulars about his early days.

1. Charles Francis Sheridan (1750–1806).
2. Elizabeth [Betsy] Hume Crawford (1758–1837), who married Henry Lefanu in 1789.
3. Sheridan attended Harrow School from 1762 to 1768.
4. During the greater part of Sheridan's stay at Harrow, his father had been compelled, by the embarrassment of his financial affairs, to reside with the remainder of the family in France, and it was at Blois that Sheridan's mother died in September 1766.
5. The Sheridan family moved to Bath in 1770.
6. On 4 May 1772, Sheridan fought a duel with Thomas Mathews, an admirer of Elizabeth Linley, who later became Sheridan's wife.

Harlequin Schoolboy*

SAMUEL PARR

With the aid of a scribe I sit down to fulfil my promise about Mr Sheridan. There was little in his boyhood worth communication. He was inferior to many of his school-fellows in the ordinary business of a school, and I do not remember any one instance in which he distinguished himself by Latin or English composition, in prose or verse.[1] Nathaniel Halhed, one of his school-fellows, wrote well in Latin and Greek.[2] Richard Archdall, another school-fellow, excelled in English verse. Richard Sheridan aspired to no rivalry with either of them. He was at the uppermost part of the fifth form, but he never reached the sixth, and, if I mistake not, he had no opportunity of attending the most difficult and the most honorable of school business,

---

* From Thomas Moore, *Memoirs of the Life of the Right Honourable Richard Brinsley Sheridan*, 5th edn (London: Longman, Hurst, Rees, Brown, Orme and Green, 1827) I, 12–14.

when the Greek plays were taught – and it was the custom at Harrow to teach these at least every year. He went through his lessons in Horace, and Virgil, and Homer well enough for a time. But, in the absence of the upper master, Doctor Sumner, it once fell in my way to instruct the two upper forms, and upon calling up Dick Sheridan, I found him not only slovenly in construing, but unusually defective in his Greek grammar. Knowing him to be a clever fellow, I did not fail to probe and to tease him. I stated his case with great good-humour to the upper master, who was one of the best tempered men in the world; and it was agreed between us, that Richard should be called oftener and worked more severely. The varlet was not suffered to stand up in his place; but was summoned to take his station near the master's table, where the voice of no prompter could reach him; and, in this defenceless condition, he was so harassed, that he at last gathered up some grammatical rules, and prepared himself for his lessons. While this tormenting process was inflicted upon him, I now and then upbraided him. But you will take notice that he did not incur any corporal punishment for his idleness: his industry was just sufficient to protect him from disgrace. All the while Sumner and I saw in him vestiges of a superior intellect. His eye, his countenance, his general manner, were striking. His answers to any common question were prompted and acute. We knew the esteem, and even admiration, which, somehow or other, all his school-fellows felt for him.[3] He was mischievous enough, but his pranks were accompanied by a sort of vivacity and cheerfulness, which delighted Sumner and myself. I had much talk with him about his apple-loft, for the supply of which all the gardens in the neighborhood were taxed, and some of the lower boys were employed to furnish it. I threatened, but without asperity, to trace the depredators, through his associates, up to their leader. He with perfect good-humor set me at defiance, and I never could bring the charge home to him. All boys and all masters were pleased with him. I often praised him as a lad of great talents, – often exhorted him to use them well; but my exhortations were fruitless. I take for granted that his taste was silently improved, and that he knew well the little which he did know. He was removed from school too soon by his father, who was the intimate friend of Sumner, and whom I often met at his house. Sumner had a fine voice, fine ear, fine taste, and, therefore, pronunciation was frequently the favorite subject between him and Tom Sheridan. I was present at many of their discussions and disputes, and sometimes took a very active part in them, – but Richard was not present. The father, you know, was a wrong-headed, whimsical man, and, perhaps his scanty circumstances were one of the reasons which prevented him from sending Richard to the University. He must have been aware, as Sumner and I were, that Richard's mind was not cast in any ordinary mould. I ought to have told you that Richard, when a boy, was a great reader of English poetry; but his exercises afforded no proof of his proficiency. In truth, he, as a boy, was quite careless about literary fame.[4] I should suppose that his father, without any regular system, polished his taste, and supplied his memory with anecdotes about our best writers in our Augustan age. The grandfather, you know, lived familiarly with Swift.[5] I have heard of him, as an excellent scholar. His boys in Ireland once performed a Greek play, and when Sir William Jones and I were talking over this event, I determined to make the experiment in England. I selected some of my best boys, and they performed the *Œdipus Tyrannus*, and the *Trachinians* of Sophocles. I wrote some Greek Iambics to vindicate myself from the imputation of singularity, and grieved I am that I did not keep a copy of them. Milton, you may remember, recommends what I attempted.

I saw much of Sheridan's father after the death of Sumner, and after my own removal from Harrow to Stanmer. I respected him, – he really liked me, and did me some important services, – but I never met him and Richard together. I often inquired about Richard, and, from the father's answers, found they were not upon good terms, – but neither he nor I ever spoke of his son's talents but in terms of the highest praise.[6]

NOTES

In 1762, Sheridan was sent to Harrow, where Dr Robert Sumner was at the head, and Dr Samuel Parr one of the under masters of the school. At Harrow, Sheridan was remarkable only as a very idle, careless, but, at the same time, engaging boy. Both Sumner and Parr endeavoured to awaken in him a consciousness of those powers, which, under all the disadvantages of indolence and carelessness, it was manifest to them that he possessed. This account of Sheridan's schooldays was written by Parr on 3 August 1818, at the request of Sheridan's biographer Thomas Moore (1779–1825), the Irish poet.

1. 'It will be seen, however, though Dr Parr was not aware of the circumstance, that Sheridan did try his talent at English verse before he left Harrow' – Moore, *Memoirs of Sheridan*, I, 12.

2. Halhend and Sheridan later collaborated on a translation or free paraphrase from the Greek, *The Love Epistles of Aristaenetus* (1771).

3. Lord Holland, however, says that Sheridan 'was slighted by the master and tormented by the boys, as a poor player's son. I have heard him relate, with tears in his eyes, that he never met with kindness at school but from Dr Parr' – *Further Memoirs of the Whig Party* (London, 1816) p. 240.

4. J. E. C. Weldon, in 'Sheridan's School Days', *The Times*, 17 Feb 1934, p. 8, observed that it is a paradox that Sheridan, who was unhappy and unpromising at Harrow, became an important literary figure.

5. The Revd Dr Thomas Sheridan (1687–1738) lives in history both as the grandfather of Richard Brinsley Sheridan and as the bosom friend of Jonathan Swift.

6. Sheridan himself remembered his schooldays at Harrow only for their misery. Cf. 'He . . . never had any scholastic fame while he was there, nor did he appear to have formed any friendships there. He said he was a very low-spirited boy, much given to crying when alone; and he attributed this very much to being neglected by his father, to his being left without money, and [to not being] taken home at the regular holidays' – Thomas Creevey, *The Creevey Papers* (London: John Murray, 1903) I, 53–4.

Sheridan at Harrow*

ALICIA LEFANU

The paternal anxiety of Mr Sheridan[1] on leaving Richard behind him,[2] for all his children were inexpressibly dear to him, was alleviated by the consideration that he was under the care of the Rev Dr Robert Sumner, his best friend. The intimacy between them began, as has been before related, during Mr Sheridan's residences at Windsor, when Dr Sumner was a master at Eton; and it was so great, that whenever Dr Sumner went up to town, and Mr Sheridan was in the country, the confidential servant left in his lodgings had orders to get them in readiness the same as for her master; and Dr Sumner made Mr Sheridan's home his temporary abode.

Dr Sumner, now head master of Harrow School, repaid this kindness by the particular attention he paid to Richard Brinsley Sheridan, who had been placed there about two years before; he had him an inmate of his house, and in every way supplied the place of a parent to him. . . .

Richard Brinsley was in some degree instructed by Dr Parr, then the first assistant in Harrow School. The care of his pecuniary concerns, in the absence of his parents, devolved on his maternal uncle, Mr Richard Chamberlaine; and though he, of course, allowed his nephew every reasonable indulgence, a little incident which happened at that time placed Richard Brinsley's love of frolic, opposed to his uncle's prudent economy, in a ludicrous point of view. On occasion of the grand annual contest for the silver arrow, Richard Brinsley was not a competitor for the prize of archery; but distinguished himself by the delivery of a Greek oration. This, as he was intended for one of the

* From *Memoirs of the Life and Writings of Mrs Frances Sheridan* (London: G. and W. B. Whittaker, 1824) pp. 251–7. Editor's title.

learned professions, was a very judicious arrangement, as it exhibited his proficiency in scholarship; and, in the embarrassed state of his father's circumstances, was far preferable to a frivolous competition, which involved a considerable degree of expense. So perhaps reasoned Mr Richard Chamberlaine; but if he did so, his nephew was determined to disappoint the old gentleman in any economical views he might have had in favouring this arrangement. The Greek oration was to be delivered in the character of a military commander; and as the notions of costume were not so strict in those days as they are at present, Richard Brinsley, of his own authority, ordered the uniform of an English general officer to be made up for the occasion. Accordingly, on the important day he appeared, not, indeed, in the elegant dress of an archer of Harrow; but in the equally expensive one of a military chief. Mr Chamberlaine, to whom of course his tailor's bill was delivered, severely remonstrated with him on this unexpected piece of extravagance. Sheridan respectfully replied, that, as the speech was to be delivered in a martial character, he did not think the effect would have been complete without an appropriate dress; and that indeed so deeply was he himself impressed with that feeling, that he was sure if he had not been properly habited, he could not have delivered a word of the oration.

What necessary connexion there was between Greek and scarlet and gold regimentals, poor Mr Chamberlaine could not exactly see; he was obliged, however, to overlook his nephew's vanity and love of shew, not without a shrewd suspicion that the pleasure of *hoaxing* him had a share in Brinsley's suddenly declared martial taste.

Mr Aikenhead, a splendid West-Indian, who had a villa at Richmond, was, with his lady, among those who, in the absence of his parents, paid the greatest attention to Richard Brinsley. This Mr Aikenhead was an old friend of Mr Sheridan's, and all the vacations of his son were spent either at the town or country residence of that gentleman, who is well known as an amateur of fashion in the literary and theatrical history of the day. If Richard Brinsley was thus beloved by his masters, school-fellows, and acquaintances, he was no less fortunate in conciliating the regard of persons in an humbler sphere: Mrs Purdon, the respectable house-keeper at Harrow, showed him, during his residence there, the attentions of a mother. After he had left school a considerable time, and was at Bath, this worthy woman had the misfortune to lose a little daughter, of whom Richard Brinsley had been remarkably fond: as a friend, who she felt assured would take an interest in her misfortune, Mrs Purdon sent Mr Sheridan on this occasion a mourning ring; and he, who was possessed of much native tenderness of heart, was greatly affected, both on hearing of the untimely death of the child, and receiving this testimony of the remembrance of his humble friend. As for Dr Sumner himself, Mr R. B. Sheridan ever remembered him with sentiments of the highest gratitude, regard and veneration; and on the death of that enlightened and distinguished man, bewailed him with the affection he owed to a second parent.

NOTES

Alicia Lefanu was Sheridan's niece.
1. Thomas Sheridan, Sheridan's father.
2. In 1764, Thomas Sheridan's financial problems continued to dog him and he decided to go with his family to live in France.

The Elopement*

ELIZABETH SHERIDAN

Her father,[1] she was certain, would at the risk of ruin to himself and his family have called the Major[2] to account, if she ventured to consult him. R. B. Sheridan sounded Mathews on the subject, and at length prevailed on him to give up the pursuit.

Miss Linley, now completely disgusted with a profession she never liked, conceived the idea of retiring to a Convent in France till she came of age, meaning to indemnify her father by giving up a part of the money settled upon her by Long.[3] She advised with her young friend Sheridan on the subject, and he communicated the scheme to his elder sister, who, thinking it meritorious to assist a young person situated as Miss Linley was in getting out of the difficulties that surrounded her, offered to give her letters of introduction to some ladies she had known in France, where she had resided some years, and Sheridan offered to be her conductor to St Quentin, where these friends lived. The arranging the whole plan of course produced frequent meetings between the young couple, and tho' Sheridan was then strongly attached to Miss Linley, he claimed only the title of friend, and his sister had no idea that the projected excursion was to lead to an immediate marriage.

At length they fixed on an evening[4] when Mr Linley, his eldest son

* From Rae, *Sheridan: A Biography*, I, 165–9. Editor's title.

and Miss M[ary] Linley were engaged at the Concert (Miss Linley being excused on the plea of illness)[5] to set out on their journey. Sheridan brought a sedan-chair to Mr Linley's house in the Crescent, in which he had Miss Linley conveyed to a post-chaise that was waiting for them on the London Road. A woman was in the chaise who had been hired by Sheridan to accompany them on this extraordinary elopement. They reached London early the next day, when Sheridan introduced Miss Linley to a friend and relation [Richard Chamberlaine], then in Town, as an Heiress who had consented to be united to him in France. Another friend [Simon Ewart], the son of a respectable brandy-merchant [John Ewart] in the City, suggested the idea of their sailing from the Port of London to Dunkirk, to which place his father had a vessel ready to sail immediately. This plan, as making a pursuit more difficult, was immediately adopted, and the old gentleman not being entirely let into the secret accompanied the young couple on board his ship, recommending them to the care of the Captain as if they had been his own children. He gave them letters of introduction to his correspondent at Dunkirk, and they were from thence given recommendations to several persons at Lille.[6]

After quitting Dunkirk, Mr Sheridan was more explicit with Miss Linley as to his views in accompanying her to France. He told her he could not be content to leave her in a Convent unless she consented to a previous marriage, which had all along been the object of his hopes, and she must be aware that, after the step she had taken, she could not appear in England but as his wife. Miss Linley, who really preferred him greatly to any person, was not difficult to persuade, and at a village not far from Calais the marriage ceremony was performed by a priest who was known to be often employed on such occasions.[7]

They then proceeded to Lille, where Miss Linley determined to stop in preference of proceeding to St Quentin. She immediately secured an apartment in a Convent, where it was settled she was to remain either till Sheridan came of age or till he was in a situation to support a wife. He remained a few days at Lille to be satisfied that she was settled to her satisfaction; but, whether from agitation of mind or fatigue, she was taken ill, and an English physician, Dr Dolman of York,[8] was called in to attend her. From what he perceived of her case he wished to have her more immediately under his care than he could in the Convent, and he and Mrs Dolman most kindly invited her to their house.[9]

NOTES

The Sheridans settled in Bath in 1770, and Richard Brinsley, while passing the time at the famous spa, chivalrously offered his assistance to the beautiful singer Elizabeth Linley (1754–1792), the toast of Bath, in her plan to flee to France to escape the unwanted attentions of an admirer and tormentor, Captain Thomas Mathews. This account was written by Elizabeth Sheridan (1758–1837), Sheridan's younger sister, at the request of Sheridan's biographer Thomas Moore. Elizabeth married Henry Lefanu in 1789.

1. Elizabeth Linley's father, Thomas Linley (1733–1795), one of the leading musicians and concert-promoters of his day.

2. Captain Thomas Mathews was one of Thomas Linley's visitors at Bath. Though a married man and much older than Elizabeth Linley, he had beguiled the simple girl into a prolonged and clandestine correspondence.

3. Elizabeth Linley's parents had forced her into an engagement with an extremely wealthy old man named Walter Long. Since Elizabeth was her father's indentured apprentice and her voice brought him considerable sums of money, Long agreed to pay £1000 in compensation for the loss of his source of income. However, according to Moore, Elizabeth told Long in secret 'that she never could be happy as his wife', whereupon he magnanimously took upon himself the burden of breaking the engagement, and closed the indignant father's mouth by settling a little fortune of £3000 upon the young lady.

4. 18 March 1772.

5. *The Bath Chronicle* shows that Thomas Linley had arranged the performance of three oratorios at Bath for the Lent of 1772, beginning with *Judas Maccabaeus* on 3 April, 'the vocal parts by Misses Linley'. An advertisement in these terms was printed in the *Bath Chronicle* for 12 and 19 March; but on 26 March Elizabeth's name was withdrawn, and only Mary's remained. It is obvious that no public performance by the Linleys was given on 18 March, and it is possible that Elizabeth Sheridan [Mrs Henry Lefanu] was confusing them with some rehearsals for the oratorios, whose production was jeopardised by Elizabeth Linley's elopement. See R. Compton Rhodes, *Harlequin Sheridan, the Man and the Legend* (Oxford: B. H. Blackwell, 1933) p. 35.

6. Another circumstantial version of the trip to Dunkirk is given by Percy Fitzgerald in *The Lives of the Sheridans* (London: R. Bentley and Son, 1886), I, 93. According to it, Elizabeth Linley and Sheridan took a boat from the Thames to Dunkirk, which was driven to Margate by stress of weather, and Cooley, the boatman, went off the next morning with other persons, by whom he was offered higher terms.

7. No other statement exists that such a ceremony did take place.

8. In York there was no 'Dr Dolman'. See Rhodes, *Harlequin Sheridan*, p. 40.

9. See also Percy Fitzgerald,'The Loves of Famous Men, No. VII: Sheridan', *Belgravia* (London), 14 (Apr 1871) 163–75, and 'Plaque to Commemorate Sheridan's Elopement', *The Times*, 6 Feb 1955, p. 10 (announces the unveiling at 11 Royal Crescent, Bath, of a plaque bearing the inscription 'Thomas Linley lived here and from this house his daughter Elizabeth eloped with Richard Brinsley Sheridan on the evening of 18th March 1772').

Announcement*

THOMAS MATHEWS

Mr Richard S[heridan] having attempted, in a letter left behind him for that purpose, to account for his scandalous method of running away from this place, by insinuations derogating from my character, and that of a young lady, innocent as far as relates to me, or my knowledge, since which he has neither taken any notice of letters, or even informed his own family of the place where he has hid himself; I cannot longer think he deserves the treatment of a gentleman, than in this public method, to post him as a L[iar], and a treacherous S[coundrel].

And as I am convinced there have been many malevolent incendiaries concerned in the propagation of this infamous lie, if any of them, unprotected by *age*, *infirmities*, or profession, will dare to acknowledge the part they have acted, and affirm *to* what they have said *of* me, they may depend on receiving the proper reward of their villainy, in the most public manner. The world will be candid enough to judge properly (I make no doubt) of any private abuse on this subject for the future; as nobody can defend himself from an accusation he is ignorant of. Thomas Mathews.

NOTE

During the absence of Sheridan and Elizabeth Linley in France, Captain Thomas Mathews continued to plague the Sheridan family with his visits and inquiries. Being dissatisfied with what he heard, he caused this violent announcement to be inserted in the *Bath Chronicle*.

* *Bath Chronicle*, 9 Apr. 1772.

Tormenting Expectation*

RICHARD BRINSLEY SHERIDAN

Dear Brother,

Most probably you will have thought me very inexcusable for not having writ to you. You will be surprised, too, to be told that, except your letter just after we arrived, we have never received one line from Bath. We suppose for certain that there are letters somewhere, in which case we shall have sent to every place almost but the right, whither, I hope, I have now sent also. You will soon see me in England. Everything on our side has at last succeeded. Miss L——[1] is now fixing in a convent, where she has been entered some time. This has been a much more difficult point than you could have imagined, and we have, I find, been extremely fortunate. She has been ill, but is now recovered;[2] this, too, has delayed me. We would have wrote, but have been kept in the most tormenting expectation, from day to day, of receiving your letters; but as everything is now so happily settled here, I will delay no longer giving you that information, though probably I shall set out for England without knowing a syllable of what has happened with you. All is well, I hope; and I hope, too, that though you may have been ignorant, for some time, of our proceedings, *you* never could have been uneasy lest anything should tempt me to depart, even in a thought, from the honor and consistency which engaged me at first. I wrote to M——[3] above a week ago, which, I think, was necessary and right. I hope he has acted the one proper part which was left to him; and, to speak from my *feelings*, I cannot but say that I shall be very happy to find no further disagreeable consequence pursuing him; for, as Brutus says of Cæsar, &c. – if I delay one moment longer, I lose the post.

I have writ now, too, to Mr Adams, and should apologize to you for having writ to him first, and lost my time for you. Love to my sisters, Miss L——[4] to all.

Ever, Charles, your affect. Brother,

R. B. Sheridan.

I need not tell you that we altered quite our route.

---

* From Moore, *Memoirs of Sheridan*, I, 51–2. Editor's title.

NOTES

Sheridan wrote this letter to his brother Charles Francis from France on 15 April 1772.
1. Elizabeth Linley.
2. Elizabeth's illness, which had been occasioned by fatigue and agitation of mind, came on some days after her retirement to the convent; but an English physician, Dr R. Dolman, who happened to be resident at Lille at the time, was called in to attend her. In order that she might be more directly under his care, he and Mrs Dolman invited her to their house, where she was found by Thomas Linley, Elizabeth's father, on his arrival in pursuit of her.
3. Thomas Mathews.
4. Mary Linley, later Mrs Tickell.

A Duel*

RICHARD BRINSLEY SHERIDAN

Mr T. Mathews thought himself injured by Mr R. Sheridan's having co-operated in the virtuous efforts of a young lady to escape the snares of vice and dissimulation. He wrote several most abusive threats to Mr S., then in France. He laboured, with a cruel industry, to vilify his character in England. He publicly posted him as a scoundrel and a liar. Mr S. answered him from France (hurried and surprised), that he should never sleep in England till he had treated him as he deserved. ... Mr S. had sat up at Canterbury, to keep his idle promise to Mr M. ... Mr S. went to Mr Cocklin's, in Crutched Friars (where Mr M. was lodged), about half after twelve. The key of Mr C.'s door was lost; Mr S. was denied admittance. By 2 o'clock he got in. ... Mr S. declares that, on Mr M.'s perceiving that he came with pistols to answer the challenge, he does not remember ever to have seen a Man behave so perfectly dastardly. ... He convinced Mr S. that his enmity might be directed solely against his brother and another gentleman at Bath. Mr S. went to Bath; in an hour he found every one of Mr M.'s assertions totally and positively disavowed. Mr S. staid but 3 hours in Bath. He returned to London. He sent to Mr M. from Hyde-parck. He came with Captain Knight his second. He objected frequently to the ground. They adjourned to the Hercules Pillars. They returned to Hyde-parck. Mr M. objected to the observation of an officer. They

* From Rae, *Sheridan: A Biography*, I, 179–82. Editor's title.

returned to Hercules Pillars. They adjourned to the Bedford Coffee-house by agreement. Mr M. was gone to the Castel Tavern. Mr S. followed with Mr E[wart]. Mr M. made many declarations in favour of Mr S. They engaged. Mr M. was disarmed, Captain Knight ran in. Mr M. begged his life and afterwards denied the advantage. Mr S. was provoked by (the really well-meant) interposition of Captain Knight and the illusion of Mr M. He insisted, since Mr M. denied the advantage, that he should give up his sword. Mr M. denied, but sooner than return to his ground he gave it up. It was broke [by Sheridan], and Mr M. [was] offered another. He was then called on to retract his abuse and beg Mr S.'s pardon. With much altercation and much ill-grace he complied. The affair was settled. The sword's being broke was not to be mentioned, if Mr M. never misrepresented the affair.[1]

NOTES

Sheridan returned to England on 28 April 1772. Thus ended the trip to France, but not its consequences. He had two *rencontres* with Captain Mathews. The first duel took place by candlelight on Monday, 4 May 1772, at the Castle Tavern in Covent Garden. The story of this duel is extremely complicated and has been told and retold, elucidated and commented, but never more admirably presented than in Sheridan's own inimitable words, drawn up hastily, it appears, at the Parade coffee-house, Bath. See Emanuel Green, *Sheridan and Mathews at Bath: A Criticism of the Story as Told in the Several Sheridan Biographies* (London: Harrison and Sons, 1912).

1. This duel resulted in an apology by Mathews which appeared in the *Bath Chronicle* of 7 May 1772. It was in the following terms: 'Being convinced that the expressions I made use of to Mr Sheridan's disadvantage was the effects of passion and misrepresentation, I retract what I have said to that gentleman's disadvantage, and particularly beg his pardon for my advertisement in the *Bath Chronicle*. Thomas Mathews.'

Proper Satisfaction*

CHARLES FRANCIS SHERIDAN

My dear Uncle, I wrote to you some time ago by Mrs Lynn and mentioned my brother's romantic expedition: he had acquitted himself

---

* From Rae, *Sheridan: A Biography*, I, 182–4. Editor's title.

in the most honourable manner, and the whole of his conduct, however imprudent it might have at first appeared, has, from the motives which influenced his undertaking, acquired him the greatest credit. But there was a circumstance I resolved never to acquaint you with till it was settled to my brother's satisfaction. This has just been done, and I shall narrate to you the whole event.

Mr Mathews, the person from whom my brother had taken Miss Linley, in a fit of rage and disappointment put an advertisement into *The Bath Chronicle* in which he publickly called him *a lyar and a treacherous scoundrel*; he not only did this but wrote to him the most impertinent letters and all upon a supposition that my brother had married Miss L[inley] and would never return to Bath. I suppose you will acknowledge it was impossible to have put up with these publick and private insults; every gentleman we were acquainted with thought it incumbent upon Dick to resent this properly, otherwise he could never show his face. But Dick's spirit did not require that the opinion of others should teach him what to do; he waited on Mr Mathews on his arrival in London; his behaviour the first visit was so very condescending that Dick let him off for a very small concession to be made in the Bath paper.

Dick on coming here for the first time saw the advertisement against him, and then thought the apology then made by M[athews] was no concession at all for so signal an insult; this being also the opinion of everybody else, he immediately resolved to return to London and get proper satisfaction. I thought it incumbent on me to accompany him to prevent mischief, if possibly consistent with his honour; we arrived in Town on Sunday (we would not call upon you as the purport of our coming must have been very disagreeable to you). I waited on M[athews] that evening, and after two hours' altercation could get him to make no further concessions. I foresaw all the disagreeable consequences attendant on coming to extremities, did all I could to prevent it, but a young man's stamping on himself the character of coward was worse than anything that could happen. They met the next day. Dick disarmed his antagonist; made him beg his life and also sign an apology to be put in the Bath paper of his own inditing; thus is the affair concluded highly to the honour of Dick, who is applauded by everyone, and whose conduct I hope you will approve of. . . . I am, my dear Uncle, your affectionate and dutiful nephew, Charles Francis Sheridan.

NOTE

In this letter to his uncle Richard Chamberlaine, Charles Francis Sheridan

(1750–1806), Sheridan's elder brother, gives his version of the encounter with Thomas Mathews. The letter is undated, but Chamberlaine noted on the back that he received it on 13 May 1772.

A Second Duel*

BATH CHRONICLE

This morning [that is, Wednesday, the day of going to press] about three o'clock, a second duel was fought with swords, between Captain Mathews and Mr R. Sheridan, on Kingsdown, near this city, in consequence of their former dispute respecting an amiable young lady,[1] which Mr M. considered as improperly adjusted; Mr S. having, since their first rencontre, declared his sentiments respecting Mr M. in a manner that the former thought required satisfaction. Mr Sheridan received three or four wounds in his breast and sides, and now lies very ill. Mr M. was only slightly wounded, and left this city soon after the affair was over.

NOTES

When Thomas Mathews returned to his estate in Wales after his defeat in the first duel, he discovered' that the reputation he had garnered in Bath had followed him, and he found himself universally shunned. Therefore, he precipitated a second duel, which took place on 1 July 1772, on Kingsdown, outside Bath.
  1. Elizabeth Linley.

* *Bath Chronicle*, Thursday, 2 July 1772.

Deepest Concern*

CHARLES FRANCIS SHERIDAN

Dear Dick, London, July 3d 1772.

It was with the deepest concern I received the late accounts of you, though it was somewhat softened by the assurance of your not being in the least danger. You cannot conceive the uneasiness it occasioned to my father. Both he and I were resolved to believe the best, and to suppose you safe, but then we neither of us could approve of the cause in which you suffer. All your friends here condemned you. You risked every thing, where you had nothing to gain, to give your antagonist the thing he wished, a chance for recovering his reputation. Your courage was past dispute: – he wanted to get rid of the contemptible opinion he was held in, and you were good-natured enough to let him do it at your expense. It is not now a time to scold, but all your friends were of opinion you could, with the greatest propriety, have refused to meet him. For my part, I shall suspend my judgement till better informed, only I cannot forgive your preferring swords.

I am exceedingly unhappy at the situation I leave you in with respect to money matters, the more so as it is totally out of my power to be of any use to you. Ewart[1] was greatly vexed at the manner of your drawing for the last 20*l*. – I own, I think with some reason.

As to old Ewart,[2] what you were talking about is absolutely impossible; he is already surprised at Mr Linley's long delay, and, indeed, I think the latter much to blame in this respect. I did intend to give you some account of myself since my arrival here,[3] but you cannot conceive how I have been hurried, – even much pressed for time at this *present writing*. I must therefore conclude, with wishing you speedily restored to heath, and that if I could make your purse as whole as that will shortly be, I hope, it would make me exceedingly happy.

I am, dear Dick, yours sincerely,

C. F. Sheridan.

---

* From Moore, *Memoirs of Sheridan*, I, 70–1. Editor's title.

NOTES

Charles Francis Sheridan (1750–1806), Sheridan's elder brother.
1. Simon Ewart.
2. John Ewart, Simon's father.
3. In May 1772, Charles Sheridan was, through the interest of a friend of his father's, appointed Secretary to the Legation in Sweden. His father, who had always been strongly attached to Charles, went to London with him to make the necessary preparations for his entering on his new situation and also to enjoy his company as long as possible.

Wonderfully Recovered*

THOMAS SHERIDAN

I did not choose to make any enquiries about the affair from my son till this morning, otherwise I should have writ to you yesterday. He is, I thank God, wonderfully recovered, and I hope he will be able to go abroad in two or three days. Some messages he received from Mathews conveyed in the most opprobrious terms, and at last a letter filled with the most scurrilous abuse, made him lose all patience and hurried him into giving him a meeting which he had before resolved against. They had not exchanged three passes before they both closed in, both fell, and both their swords were broke. But my son's snapped across within four inches of the hilt and that of Mr Mathews was only shivered in the middle, leaving a jagged point and running tapering up a great way of the blade.

At first my son had the advantage in the fall, having thrown Mathews down, but as the ground happened to be sloping where they fell, the other rolled over him, and got uppermost. My son called out that he had nothing to defend himself with; the other holding the pointed part of the sword over him, which he had picked up from the ground, bid him beg his life. My son said he never would beg his life from such a scoundrel; Mathews then began to stab him, and my son after the first wound caught hold of one part of it, so as that the other could not disengage it. He then proceeded to stab him with the jagged pointed sword which he held in the other hand, uttering horrid curses all the while. It is said that the number of stabs which he made as quick as possible, could not be less than twenty or thirty; my son had the good

---

* From Rae, *Sheridan: A Biography*, I, 203–5. Editor's title.

fortune to put by most of them with his hand, so that they only penetrated his coat, but five of them took place, fortunately all flesh wounds, having been stopped by the bones. Mathews then went off swearing he had done for him.

Never was more concern shown on any occasion than was here to be seen in all classes of people on my son's account; for he bears an excellent character; and is much beloved. And never were more execrations poured upon any head than that of the vile assassin. Never was a man so universally detested, and I do verily believe were he to appear in the streets of Bath by day, he would be stoned to death by the populace. If ever he should show his head here again he will be shunned as one infected by the plague. I have not time to say anything more, but hereafter you shall have farther particulars. If Charles[1] should be detained in London, tell him I expect to hear from him. My love to the little woman. All my young folks join in love and duty to you both.[2]

NOTES

Thomas Sheridan (1719–1788), Sheridan's father, was an actor, elocutionist, lexicographer, and writer on education. He gave his version of what had occurred in a letter to his brother-in-law Richard Chamberlaine, which was written on 9 July 1772. See Esther K. Sheldon, *Thomas Sheridan of Smock-Alley* (Princeton, NJ: Princeton University Press, 1967).

1. Charles Francis Sheridan.
2. On 14 May 1821, Lord Thanet told Thomas Moore that 'Lord John Townshend and (I think) Hare went to Bath for the purpose of getting acquainted with Mathews, and making inquiries about his affair with Sheridan. Mathews described the duel as a mere hoax – in fact, no duel at all; that Sheridan came drunk, and that he (Mathews) could have killed him with the greatest ease if he had chosen.' Moore adds, 'A precious fellow this Mathews was!' Thomas Moore, *Memoirs, Journals, and Correspondence*, ed. Lord John Russell (London: Longman, Brown, Green, and Longmans, 1853–6) III, 233.

No, by God, I Won't*

WILLIAM BARNETT

On quitting our chaises at the top of Kingsdown, I entered into a conversation with Captain Paumier,[1] relative to some preliminaries I thought ought to be settled in an affair which was likely to end very seriously; – particularly the method of using their pistols, which Mr Mathews had repeatedly signified his desire to use prior to swords, from a conviction that Mr Sheridan would run in on him, and an ungentlemanlike scuffle probably be the consequence. This, however, was refused by Mr Sheridan, declaring he had no pistols: Captain Paumier replied he had a brace (which I know were loaded). – By my advice, Mr Mathews's were not loaded, as I imagined it was always customary to load on the field, which I mentioned to Captain Paumier at the White-Hart, before we went out, and desired he would draw his pistols. He replied, as they were already loaded, and the going on a public road at that time of the morning, he might as well let them remain so, till we got to the place appointed, when he would on his honor draw them, which I am convinced he would have done had there been time; but Mr Sheridan immediately drew his sword, and, in a vaunting manner, desired Mr Mathews to draw (their ground was very uneven, and near the post-chaises). – Mr Mathews drew; Mr Sheridan advanced on him at first; Mr Mathews in turn advanced fast on Mr Sheridan; upon which he retreated, till he very suddenly ran in upon Mr Mathews, laying himself exceedingly open, and endeavoring to get hold of Mr Mathews's sword; Mr Mathews received him on his point, and, I believe, disengaged his sword from Mr Sheridan's body, and gave him another wound; which, I suppose, must have been either against one of his ribs, or his breast-bone, as his sword broke, which I imagine happened from the resistance it met with from one of those parts; but whether it was broke by that, or on the closing, I cannot aver.

Mr Mathews, I think, on finding his sword broke, laid hold of Mr Sheridan's sword-arm, and tripped up his heels: they both fell; Mr Mathews was uppermost, with the hilt of his sword in his hand, having about six or seven inches of the blade to it, with which I saw him give

---

* Copy of a paper left by William Barnett in the hands of Captain William Wade, master of ceremonies at Bath; repr. in Moore, *Memoirs of Sheridan*, I, 63–5. Editor's title.

Mr Sheridan, as I imagined, a skin-wound or two in the neck; for it could be no more, – the remaining part of the sword being broad and blunt; he also beat him in the face either with his fist or the hilt of his sword. Upon this I turned from them, and asked Captain Paumier if we should not take them up; but I cannot say whether he heard me or not, as there was a good deal of noise; however, he made no reply. I again turned to the combatants, who were much in the same situation: I found Mr Sheridan's sword was bent, and he slipped his hand up the small part of it, and gave Mr Mathews a slight wound in the left part of his belly: I that instant turned again to Captain Paumier, and proposed again our taking them up. He in the same moment called out, 'Oh! he is killed, he is killed!' – I as quick as possible turned again, and found Mr Mathews had recovered the point of his sword, that was before on the ground, with which he had wounded Mr Sheridan in the belly: I saw him drawing the point out of the wound. By this time Mr Sheridan's sword was broke, which he told us. – Captain Paumier called out to him, 'My dear Sheridan, beg your life, and I will be yours for ever.' I also desired him to ask his life: he replied, 'No, by God, I won't.' I then told Captain Paumier it would not do to wait for those punctilios (or words to that effect), and desired he would assist me in taking them up. Mr Mathews most readily acquiesced first, desiring me to see Mr Sheridan was disarmed. I desired him to give me the tuck, which he readily did, as did Mr Sheridan the broken part of his sword to Captain Paumier. Mr Sheridan and Mr Mathews both got up; the former was helped into one of the chaises, and drove off for Bath, and Mr Mathews made the best of his way for London.

The whole of this narrative I declare, on the word and honour of a gentleman, to be exactly true; and that Mr Mathews discovered as much genuine, cool, and intrepid resolution as man could do.

I think I may be allowed to be an impartial relater of facts, as my motive for accompanying Mr Mathews was no personal friendship, (not having any previous intimacy, or being barely acquainted with him,) but from a great desire of clearing up so ambiguous an affair, without prejudice to either party, – which a stranger was judged the most proper to do, – particularly as Mr Mathews had been blamed before for taking a relation with him on a similar occasion.

(Signed)   William Barnett.

October, 1772.

NOTES

William Barnett was Captain Thomas Mathews' second in this duel. He was the one who had manipulated the second duel.
1. Sheridan's second.

Playful Talent*

HENRY ANGELO

As I have heard my father and mother say, and as I have repeated, Garrick[1] could not endure to see his amiable spouse 'trip it on the light fantastic toe'; neither could young Sheridan endure to hear his sweet bride, 'warble her native wood-notes wild'; though, to do justice to her memory, art had amply improved her strains. Some few months after their nuptials,[2] our family, the Linleys, and Willoughby Lacy, spent an evening at Christmas, at Richard Brinsley's house, in Orchard-street.[3] We kept it up to a late hour; and music making part of the after-supper entertainment, Mamma Linley[4] asked her daughter to sing a certain little favourite air; but a single glance from her juvenile lord and master, kept her mute.[5]

With reference to these family appeals, however, my father and mother happily steered so friendly a course, that no ill will ensued; and their joint efforts, contributed, by good management, to heal the wounded feelings of these very worthy parties, and bring about a reconciliation.

Among innumerable instances of the playful talent and ready wit of Richard, or as he was more familiarly addressed by our family, *Dick* Sheridan, I must relate one, which though happening long ago, appears but recent, from my just pouncing upon the printed document, in rummaging amidst my stores of literary scraps, which I shall subjoin.

This relates to the splendid masquerade which was given at the Pantheon, soon after that superb structure, the first great effort of the science of the late James Wyatt, was opened to the public.[6] This magnificent building was then in the zenith of its glory. My father, on more than one public occasion, was appointed honorary master of the ceremonies at this resort of high fashion. On this, however, he went merely as a visitor, in character. The preceding day, my father

---

* Henry Angelo, *Reminiscences* (London: Henry Colburn and Richard Bentley, 1830) I, 87–90. Editor's title.

entertained a dinner party, when the masquerade being the subject of conversation, it became a general question what character the elder Angelo should assume. 'You, who have made so conspicuous a figure in the Carnival, at Venice,' said the elder Sheridan, 'must shine in an English mumming.' Many characters were suggested, when my father, at the instance of my mother, chose that of a mountebank conjuror. This being settled, in complaisance to the lady hostess, by general acclamation, Richard Brinsley said, 'Come, Doctor Angelo, give me pen, ink, and paper, and I will furnish you with a card to distribute to the motley crowd, who will surround you.' The materials produced, he wrote the following *jeu d'esprit*,[7] talking, laughing, and entering into the chit-chat, all the while he composed it.

'A CONJUROR. – Just arrived in the Haymarket, from the very extremity of Hammersmith (where he has spent a number of years in a two pair of stairs lodging), *A most noted and extraordinary Conjuror*, having visited above nine different Parishes in the space of a fortnight, and had the honour of exhibiting before most of the Churchwardens between Knightsbridge and Brentford.

'It is not in the power of words (unless some new language were invented for the purpose) to describe the extraordinary feats he performs.

'He takes a glass of wine (provided it be good), and, though you should fill it up to the very brim, he will drink it off – with the greatest ease and satisfaction.

'He makes no scruple of eating a plate of cold ham and chicken, if it be supper time – before the face of the whole company.

'Any gentleman or lady may lend him five or six guineas, which he puts into his pocket – and never returns if he can help it.

'He takes a common pocket handkerchief out of his pocket, rumples it in his hand, blows his nose, and returns it into his pocket again, with the most astonishing composure.

'When gentlemen are talking on any subject on which there appears a difference of opinion, he joins in the conversation, or holds his tongue – just as it happens.

'Any nobleman, gentleman, or lady may look him full in the face, and – see whether they know him or not.

'In short, it would appear quite incredible to enumerate the unheard-of qualities he possesses, and the unprecedented wonders he performs; and all for his own private emolument, and for no other motive or consideration whatever!'

This was immediately dispatched to the printers in Wardour-street, and five hundred copies were composed, and struck off, dried, pressed, and ready by twelve at night, which was considered a great effort of the press in those days, printing then not being dispatched, as now, by the miraculous expedition of a steam-engine of thirty horse power.

NOTES

After his wife's death in 1766, Thomas Sheridan took a house in Frith Street, Soho. His *Plan of Education for the Young Nobility and Gentry of Great Britain* was published that year in Dublin and later in London. A pupil of his at this time was the young Henry Angelo, whose father, the great swordsman, in exchange for his son's instruction, provided lessons in riding and fencing for both Charles Francis and Richard Brinsley in his Soho Academy.

1. David Garrick (1717–79), English actor who became manager of Drury Lane Theatre in 1747. He is regarded as one of the greatest actors in the history of the English stage.
2. Sheridan married Elizabeth Linley on 13 April 1773.
3. After their marriage, Sheridan and his wife lived for a while in a cottage at Burnham Grove, and then moved to a house in Orchard Street in the spring of 1774.
4. Mary Linley, née Johnson (1729–1820), Elizabeth Linley's mother.
5. Sheridan grandly scorned in his poverty to revel in idle luxury upon the large income which his wife could easily have earned. The cynics of his day considered him Quixotic. Dr Samuel Johnson eulogised Sheridan for withdrawing his wife from a profession in which she appeared in public.
6. The Pantheon, that 'much-talked-of Receptacle of fashionable Pleasure' in Oxford Street, opened in 1772.
7. Humorous trifle, usually literary.

The Rivals *

MARY LINLEY

My dearest Eliza, Bath.

We are all in the greatest anxiety about Sheridan's play, – though I do not think there is the least doubt of its succeeding. I was told last night that it was his own story, and therefore called *The Rivals*;[1] but I do not give any credit to this intelligence. . . .

I am told he will get at least 700*l.* for his play.

Bath, January, 1775.

It is impossible to tell you what pleasure we felt at the receipt of

* From Moore, *Memoirs of Sheridan*, I, 93–4.

Sheridan's last letter, which confirmed what we had seen in the newspapers of the success of his play. The *knowing ones* were very much disappointed, as they had so very bad an opinion of its success. After the first night we were indeed all very fearful that the audience would go very much prejudiced against it. But now, there can be no doubt of its success, as it has certainly got through more difficulties than any comedy which has not met its doom the first night. I know you have been very busy in writing for Sheridan, – I don't mean *copying*, but *composing*; – it's true, indeed; – you must not contradict me when I say you wrote the much admired epilogue to *The Rivals*.[2] How I long to read it! What makes it more certain is, that my *father* guessed it was *yours* the first time he saw it praised in the paper.

NOTES

Mary Linley [later Mrs Richard Tickell] (1758–1787) wrote these letters to her sister Elizabeth, Sheridan's wife.

1. *The Rivals*, Sheridan's first play, was produced at Covent Garden Theatre, London, on 17 January 1775, and was withdrawn immediately after the first night for alterations. The revised version was presented on 28 January 1775.

2. This statement respecting the epilogue proves only the high idea entertained of Elizabeth Sheridan by her own family. On the Linleys see Clementina Black, *The Linleys of Bath* (London: Martin Secker, 1911; rev. edn Miller, 1971); Margot Bor and Lamond Clellend, *Still the Lark: A Biography of Elizabeth Linley* (London: Merlin Press, 1962); and Roger Fiske, 'The Linleys 1775–1780', in *English Theatre Music in the Eighteenth Century* (Oxford: Oxford University Press, 1973) pp. 413–21.

*The Duenna**

THOMAS LINLEY

I have promised to assist Sheridan in compiling – I believe this is the properest term – an opera, which I understand from him he has engaged to produce at Covent Garden this season. I have already set some airs which he has given me, and he intends writing new words to some tunes of mine. My son[1] has likewise written some tunes for him,

---

* From Lloyd C. Sanders, *Life of Richard Brinsley Sheridan* (London: Walter Scott, 1890) pp. 47–8. Editor's title.

and I understand he is to have some others from Mr Jackson of Exeter. This is a mode of proceeding in regard to his composition which I by no means approve of. I think he ought first to have finished his opera with the songs he intends to introduce into it, and have got it entirely new set. No musician can set a song properly unless he understands the character and knows the performer who is to exhibit it. . . . I would not have been concerned in this business at all, but that I know there is an absolute necessity for him to endeavour to get some money by this means, and he will not be persuaded upon to let his wife sing,[2] and indeed at present she is incapable, and nature will not permit me to be indifferent to his success.

NOTES

All through the summer of 1775 Sheridan worked hard at a comic opera, the music for which was selected and composed by his father-in-law, Thomas Linley (1733–95). The pair conducted their labours chiefly by correspondence, as Linley had a professional engagement at Bath. Although Sheridan had no technical training in music, yet he displayed much practical knowledge of its effect upon the stage. No doubt he was helped to a very considerable extent by his accomplished wife Elizabeth, as it will be observed that Sheridan, in his directions to Linley, speaks in the plural more often than in the singular. *The Duenna* was performed at Covent Garden Theatre on 21 November 1775. It had an unprecedented run of seventy-five nights in its first season (as against the sixty-three of *The Beggar's Opera*), and amassed some 254 performances in the eighteenth century. This letter, in which Thomas Linley vents his feelings, is addressed to David Garrick.

1. Tom Linley (1756–78).
2. When Sheridan married Elizabeth Linley in 1773, she was the most admired singer of her day, but from the beginning of their married life she and Sheridan agreed that she should no longer sing in public.

The School for Scandal *

FREDERIC REYNOLDS

. . . on the first night of *The School for Scandal*, returning from Lincoln's Inn, about nine o'clock, and passing through the Pit passage, from

* Frederic Reynolds, *Life and Times* (London, 1826) I, 110. Editor's title.

Vinegar-yard to Brydges Street, I heard such a tremendous noise over my head, that, fearing the Theatre was proceeding to fall about it, I ran for my life; but found, the next morning, that the noise did not arise from the *falling* of the house, but from the *falling* of the screen, in the fourth act; so violent, and so tumultuous were the applause and laughter.

NOTE

Frederic Reynolds (1764–1841), English dramatist, records the success of *The School for Scandal*, which was produced at Drury Lane Theatre on 8 May 1777.

By My Own Son*

THOMAS SHERIDAN

At length a scene opened which promised better days. Garrick's retiring,[1] whose jealousy had long shut the London theatres against me, such an opening was made for me, both as manager and actor as might soon have retrieved my affairs, and in no long space of time have placed me in easy circumstances. But here a son of mine steps into possession, whose first step was to exclude me wholly from having any share in it.

Afterwards, when by extreme ill-conduct they were threatened with ruin, he agreed to put the management into my hands upon condition that I should not appear as a performer, and in this he got his brother managers to join him with such earnestness that merely to gratify him I acquiesced.

I desire to know whether if the theatre of Drury Lane had fallen into the hands of the worst enemy I had in the world, determined upon ruining me and my family, he could have taken more effectual means of doing it than those which have been pursued by my own son?

NOTES

'Thomas was inevitably his own worst enemy. He hated Johnson for his fame

* From Rae, *Sheridan: A Biography*, II, 4. Editor's title.

over his Dictionary, certain that he himself had written a far better one. He considered himself to be Garrick's equal as an actor. And he was certain that, had he been given the chance, he could have reformed the entire educational system in England and Ireland. He was a man of some skills, but the troubles and disasters which he had undergone in Ireland had warped his character; and the early loss of his wife removed an influence which could, perhaps, have softened his view of the world. By 1778, although he had somewhat recovered from his huff and did join the company, he still smarted from the ban on his acting' – Madeleine Bingham, *Sheridan: The Track of a Comet* (London: George Allen and Unwin, 1972) p. 151. Thomas's bitterness at this period is well reflected in this letter to his son Charles dated 15 April 1783, some time after the events had occurred.

1. In June 1776, David Garrick retired from the stage, and Richard Brinsley Sheridan signed the agreement which made over Garrick's half of Drury Lane Theatre to himself and two partners. In 1778, he acquired the remaining half-share in Drury Lane.

Sheridan and Cumberland*

STANLEY THOMAS WILLIAMS

Although Garrick had already retired from the stage, he was evidently persuaded by Cumberland to interest himself in *The Battle of Hastings*. Universal mender-of-plays as he was, he corrected, revised, and amended until Cumberland mustered courage to present the play to Sheridan, then the newly made manager of Drury Lane Theatre. It is said that the leader of sentimental comedy was introduced to Sheridan by a letter from Garrick. Soon we learn of Cumberland's begging the new manager to stage his tragedy.

Sheridan's facile genius was not yet at its height, but youth, consciousness of great powers, and a capricious temperament, made him rule Drury Lane without mercy. His treatment of Cumberland exhibits the arrogance of a dictator. A number of letters exist, showing the lengths to which Cumberland went to obtain a hearing for his new play. The first of these is an humble one, asking Sheridan to give the tragedy his consideration. 'I ought and should have despaired of its merits,' writes Cumberland, 'if I had not had a pretty long and intimate acquaintance with the stage, and what produces stage effect; if I had

---

* Stanley Thomas Williams, *Richard Cumberland: His Life and Dramatic Works* (New Haven, Conn.: Yale University Press; London: Oxford University Press, 1917) pp. 137–50. Editor's title.

not given infinite pains and attention to this composition for many years; and, above all, if I had not been supported by the unanimous suffrages of every person to whose judgment I have committed it.' After this account of the tragedy, Cumberland says, with abjectness enough to satisfy the most tyrannical manager, and with an offer to dispense with the honorarium: 'I beseech you, therefore, Sir, to read it with as much malice as you are capable of, considering that an author is an ill judge in his own cause.'[1]

To this epistle Sheridan did not apparently reply. The evasive Colman[2] had asked about the fate of the tragedy, and Cumberland says: 'I was forced to add, that having written a letter on Friday se'nnight to Mr Sheridan in the most candid and fair terms I could devise, he had not to this moment acknowledged the receipt of it.'[3] At this treatment Cumberland's irritation showed through his customary veneer of politeness. 'We both agreed,' he says referring to Sheridan, 'that such a conduct must be altered, or it would operate to his ruin. . . . My experience with the world assures me that there is no man who can keep his place in the good will and esteem of those he has to deal with, *if he so totally throws off the forms of politeness*.'[4] Cumberland was assuredly in the right, and Fitzgerald, in his *Lives of the Sheridans*, convicts Sheridan of unpardonable rudeness in his treatment of the playwright.[5]

In the end Sheridan accepted the play. Then followed a tumultuous season of rehearsal and preparation. Sheridan loathed the heavy tragedy; the performers had no confidence in it; and Garrick regretted his intercession. Under the actor's pen, revision and deletion continued. We have Cumberland's piqued thanks for Garrick's candid opinion of an epilogue. The author encloses another, fortified with a host of apologies. It was written, he swears, 'post-haste directly upon reading Garrick's letter'. For other suggestions from his friend the dramatist is eternally grateful. Meanwhile Sheridan's cool insolence tortures Cumberland, and the entire correspondence reflects the perturbed nerves of all connected with the unfortunate play. Although he boasts of its submission, the dramatist's temper hangs by a thread: 'We have', he writes Garrick, 'as yet had no rehearsal, nor can I tell when we shall. . . . Without some prudence and patience I should never have got the ladies cordially into their business, nor should I not only have avoided a jar with Mr Smith, but so far have impressed him in my favour as to draw an offer from him (though too late) of taking the part of *Edwin*.' A petulant postscript adds: 'No news whatever. Pray burn the copy of my epilogue.'[6]

Sheridan's indifference to Cumberland and to his tragedies is clear in a letter from the latter to Garrick: 'I read', writes Cumberland, 'the tragedy in the ears of the performers on Friday morning; I was highly flattered by my audience, but your successor in management is not a representative of your polite attention to authors on such occasions, *for he came in yawning at the fifth act*, with no other apology than having sate up two nights running.'[7] Garrick has evidently cautioned Cumberland against offending Sheridan, for Cumberland writes with some complacence: 'Thank you for your advice; I persuade myself I have anticipated it, and shall certainly not lose the battle for want of temper.'[8] On another day he has 'called ... on Mr Sheridan and quickened him, but all in good humour and perfect harmony'.[9] A letter, written presumably the next evening, is still more hopeful: 'I have this morning, my dear friend, rehearsed the "Battle", and a brave battle we made. Madam Yates rehearsed without book her whole part; all was harmony, zeal, and good will: nothing lagged or hobbled in the whole; and the new corrections (especially the *finale* to the fourth act) were applauded. The fifth act, which was long, is now very brilliant, and I am well contented to take my trial.'[10]

Since Garrick had formed *The Battle of Hastings*, this turn for the better must have pleased him. It is certain that he was interested in *The Battle of Hastings*, but whether from real belief in its worth, or from a desire to befriend Cumberland, is uncertain. 'It has been said', remarks Davies,[11] 'that Mr Garrick, after he had left the stage, recommended *The Battle of Hastings* to Mr Sheridan with great warmth, from an earnest desire to oblige the author, who, on this occasion did not seem to have a proper sense of Mr Garrick's friendship. . . .' The patron was noncommittal in expressing an opinion of the play: 'Mr Garrick was asked by several persons his judgment of that tragedy; his constant answer was, *Sir, what all the world says, must be true.* No explanation of his meaning could be drawn from him.'[12] It is, in all events, clear that Garrick was disgusted with the correspondence relative to *The Battle of Hastings*, for we find at the end of this a bit of damning evidence: 'Endorsed, Mr Cumberland's letters to me when at Althorp, in Dec. 1777, about *The Battle of Hastings*; – a true picture of the man.'[13]

So the weeks passed, and, more than two years after it was written, on January 24, 1778, at Drury Lane Theatre, *The Battle of Hastings* was acted. It had been ushered into the world only by the persistence of Cumberland; Sheridan and Garrick stood by, disgusted sponsors, disliking more than ever both the play and Cumberland himself. The play was acted twelve times, but real success was despaired of from the first. Friendly comments were few, though George Cumberland wrote his brother, Richard Denison Cumberland, that even if 'no friend to slaughter and destruction', he thought it a 'pleasing tragedy'.[14] The critique of *The Town and Country Magazine* for January was, perhaps, the most tolerant: '*The Battle of Hastings* is very far from being a contemptible production; and, with the aid of a pruning knife . . . we hope to see it in far greater perfection.' Such tributes seem rare in the storm of universal vituperation. 'Why', says *Scot's Magazine* for February, 'Mr Cumberland has chosen to call this play *The Battle of Hastings*, we do not see. To be sure we hear something of such a battle in the last act, but almost the whole of the tragedy consists of love-scenes between a disguised prince, and a couple of fond maidens. The Rival Beauties would have been a more proper name for it. The French are blamed for filling their tragedies with love; Mr Cumberland appears inclined to keep them in countenance.'

When, some thirty years before, Cumberland had given to Doctor Nicolls of Westminster a set of plagiarized verses, his school-fellows had smiled. Later the critics of *The Brothers* and *The West Indian* had discovered in these plays scenes and lines of a strongly allusive character. But in *The Battle of Hastings* all previous faults of this nature were transcended. The plot has echoes from all sentimental comedy, and the language is steeped in the diction of Shakespeare. Here was an opportunity for the critics to annihilate their enemy. The reviewer of *St James Chronicle* of January 20 allows himself to be satirical: 'The story *is* wonderful; the Incidents all calculated to startle, and the language all Daisies and Lilies and Pinks and Roses. The Slips and Roots of most of them have been stolen; but from a Garden where they will not be missed, and Author and Connoisseurs may be guilty of Stealing and not of Felony.' *The London Review* has many malicious references to 'Squire Cumberland'. Later commentators have been equally severe.

'The coat of Joseph,' says *Biographia Dramatica*, 'and the dress of Harlequin, were never composed of patchwork more general than is the style of this performance. An injudicious application of Shakespeare's phraseology throughout all parts of it, continually provokes a comparison unfavourable to our present author. Add to this, that he has grossly violated the truth of history, in his representations of Edgar Atheling and Harold. Under his hand they may be said to have exchanged characters. ... It was cooly received.'[15] 'A strange incongruous business',[16] says the unfriendly Dibdin, and Davies declares that '*The Battle of Hastings* is what we call a Pasticio, a work made up of centos from various authors, and more particularly from Shakespeare.'[17]

The Battle of Hastings has all the faults of bad tragedy, and is, as Doran says, 'as near Shakespeare as Ireland's *Vortigern*',[18] a play hissed from the stage on the first night. The play fails today, as in 1778, by any dramatic test, yet has, rising from its worst vice, one virtue. Out of long periods of stiff, impossible diction occasionally sounds the beat of sonorous and melodious verse. 'The language,' says Scott, 'often uncommonly striking, has more merit than the characters or the plot.'[19]

The failure of *The Battle of Hastings* justified Sheridan's ridicule of the tragedy, and confirmed his impression of the play and of its author. His feelings towards Cumberland now verged upon hearty contempt; nor was he without resentment and anger. It is improbable that Sheridan had forgotten the sharp reflections upon his friends in Cumberland's farce, *The Note of Hand*; moreover, other events had increased his irritation against the dramatist to the breaking point. In his *Memoirs of Sheridan* Watkins says:

> What was the cause of the quarrel between Mr Sheridan and Mr Cumberland has never been clearly stated; but the generally accepted story at the time was that the former, in his capacity of manager, rejected every piece Cumberland offered at Drury Lane, which occasioned some sharp language on both sides; and as other literary persons had similar complaints against the conduct of the manager, a common concern was made of the injury, and the newspapers daily exhibited some severe criticisms upon theatrical subjects and the direction of Drury Lane.[20]

Sheridan's disgust with Cumberland was doubtless increased by stories of Cumberland's depreciation of *The School for Scandal*, when it appeared in 1777. The miscellanies called *Sheridaniana* give the best narration of this popular, but probably apocryphal, tale of the time: 'When *The School for Scandal* came out, Cumberland's children prevailed upon their father to take them to see it; – they had the stage-box – their father was seated behind them; and as the story was told by a gentleman, a friend of Sheridan's, who was close by, every time the children laughed at what was going on on the stage, he pinched them, and said, "What are you laughing at, my dear little folks? You should not laugh, my angels; there is nothing to laugh at", and then, in an undertone, "keep still, you little dunces". Sheridan having been told of this long afterwards, said, "It was very ungrateful in Cumberland to have been displeased with his poor children for laughing at *my comedy*; for I went the other night to see *his tragedy*, and laughed at it from beginning to end."'.[21]

There were many other stories of Cumberland's unhappiness at the success of *The School for Scandal*. A rumour reached Sheridan's ear that Cumberland had sneered at the play in the lobby of the theatre, on its first night. 'I gave my accuser proof positive', Cumberland says, in a tone of rather loud protest, 'that I was at Bath during the time of its first run, never saw it during its first season, and exhibited my pocket-journal in confirmation of my alibi: the gentleman was convinced of my innocence, but as he had no opportunity of correcting his libel, every body that read it remains convinced of my guilt.'

Whether or not Sheridan had heard of Cumberland's 'd—d disinheriting countenance' at *The School for Scandal* it is evident that he was irritated at Cumberland some time before the acting of *The Critic*, for both dramatists were supersensitive, and it is likely that the jarring relations fomented a busy malice in Sheridan's mind, which reached its climax in the immortal Sir Fretful.[22] Sheridan's desire for revenge because of real or fancied affronts admits of no doubt. 'To defend himself,' says *The Westminster Magazine* for November, 1779, 'and to be revenged on his enemies, he has brought forth *The Critick*, in which he has *preached*, and caricatured his old Friends most outrageously.' *The Critical Review* for December, 1779, thinks that Sheridan is 'exceedingly angry with the ministry of our theatrical world, and endeavours, though with no great dexterity, to hold them forth to the ridicule and indignation of the public'. *The St James Chronicle* of March 3, 1779, after a review of Sheridan's dispute with certain 'play writers', says that the author of *The Critic* has forgotten their flattery, and now attacks them. 'The first Act . . . is seemingly and tenderly directed at News-Papers and Criticks, but most pointedly against Dramatic Writers, *who are the Authors very good friends*.'

That Cumberland was the model from whom Sir Fretful Plagiary was drawn, has been the belief since the first performance of *The Critic*. 'Sir Fretful Plagiary', says *The Town and Country Magazine* for November, 1779, 'is drawn with a bold pencil, and the original may easily be traced by the striking features of the copy', and *Lloyd's Evening Post* of November 1, 1779, calls him 'a character whose outline is so . . . drawn "that he who runs may read him!"' *The Lady's Magazine* for November of the same year, says: 'Sir Fretful Plagiary is soon after announced, and exhibits one of the most harsh and severe caricatures that has been attempted since the days of Aristophanes, of which a celebrated sentimental writer is evidently the object; a great part of what is said by his representative being literally taken from his usual conversation, but with very pointed and keen additions.' Watkins in his *Memoirs of Sheridan* declares 'that Cumberland was the principal object at whom the shaft of ridicule was directed, could not be doubted by any who were acquainted with that gentleman and his writings; and Mr Sheridan, so far from disguising his intention in the application, took every opportunity, in public and private, of expressing his satisfaction at the mortification which it produced.'[23]

Later critics echoed this opinion. Sir Fretful, says Adolphus, '. . . was a personal representation of a well-known living dramatist',[24] and William Earle adds that 'the character of Sir Fretful Plagiary was intended as a broad satire and faithful hit upon the strange peculiarities of Richard Cumberland'.[25]

That Sheridan was, in one or two places, thinking of his experience of *The Battle of Hastings* in his sketch of Sir Fretful Plagiary, can hardly be doubted. *The Critic* was produced but a year after the tragedy, with the history of its unhappy juggling between the two theatres, and its miserable failure, fresh in Sheridan's mind. 'I sent it to the manager of Covent Garden Theatre this morning', says Sir Fretful of his play. If the story of Sheridan's laughter at *The Battle of Hastings* is true, the author of *The Critic* was doubtless thinking of this tragedy when he makes Sir Fretful say: 'Why, sir, for aught I know, he might take out some of the best things in my tragedy, and put them into his own comedy.' References to plagiarisms from Shakespeare would never be so likely as after familiarity with this particular tragedy. 'Your imitations of Shakespeare', says Sneer to Sir Fretful, 'resemble the mimicry of Falstaff's page, and are about as near the standard of the original.'[26]

It is not, however, certain that Sheridan had Cumberland exclusively in mind when he created the character. In his capacity as manager, it is probably that many a tiresome playwright ruffled his nerves. At this very time he was at swords' points with Colman, and it is quite possible that the first act of *The Critic* satirises types rather than individuals. The conclusion follows naturally that the sketch of Sir Fretful Plagiary may be eclectic, and that Cumberland, Colman, and their brother dramatists all contributed features for the portrait. That Cumberland was the man, says one critic, 'Sheridan has almost given his assent'.[27] Such a criticism virtually says to the world, 'You may call this figure Cumberland, if you wish', and has rather the air of naming a composite photograph after its completion, than of having reproduced a definite man. 'Whether Sir *Fretful Plagiary* is drawn from Nature, or is only the Coinage of Fancy, we will not determine', says *The Public Advertiser* of November 1, 1779, and in a collection of dramatic data called *The Eccentricities of John Edwin*, published in 1791, occurs a passage which may approximate truth in the matter: 'The common idea that Sir FRETFUL PLAGIARY was intended as a satire on Mr CUMBERLAND is fallacious, as no particular person was alluded to – Some of the performers imagining it was a satire on the *elder* COLMAN, Mr SHERIDAN expressed a wish that it should rather be considered as a likeness of CUMBERLAND, both characters having openly affected to treat the newspaper Editors with contempt, while they secretly trembled at their power.'[28]

Whether or not he was the original of Sir Fretful, Cumberland paid a bitter penalty for a temperament which allied him instantly to the caricature. It is said that one of his sons was the first to recognize him, and his name is inseparably linked with a rôle which has appeared on almost every stage. His incarnation for theatre-goers by a skilful actor is best described by Boaden: 'It was perhaps reserved for Sheridan to show the utmost that Parsons could achieve, in Sir Fretful Plagiary in the *Critic*. I have repeatedly enjoyed this rich treat, and become sensible how painful laughter might be, when such a man as Parsons chose to throw his whole force into a character. When he stood under the castigation of Sneer, affecting to enjoy criticisms, which made him writhe in agony; when the tears were in his eyes, and he suddenly checked his unnatural laugh, to enable him to stare aghast upon his tormentors; a picture was exhibited of mental anguish and frantic rage, or mortified vanity and affected contempt which would almost deter an author from the pen, unless he could be sure of his firmness under every possible provocation.'[29]

Sir Fretful was also a popular part of Charles Mathews's.[30] Walter Scott describes the acting of Sir Fretful Plagiary by Mathews. On January 9, 1826, the novelist wrote: 'Mathews last night gave us a very perfect imitation of old Cumberland, who carried the poetic jealousy and irritability further than any man I ever saw.'[31] But Scott says also: 'It is not from a caricature that a just picture can be drawn, and in the little pettish sub-acidity of temper which Cumberland sometimes exhibited, there was more of humourous sadness than of ill-will.'[32] Cumberland does not mention Sir Fretful Plagiary in the *Memoirs*, and we can only imagine the pain it gave his sensitive nature.

Cumberland, on his side, seems to have felt a respect for Sheridan not discernible in his attitude towards Goldsmith or his other contemporaries. 'I could', he says, 'name one living, who has made such happy use of his screen in a comedy of the first merit, that if Aristotle himself had written a whole chapter professedly against screens, and Jerry Collier had edited it with notes and illustrations, I would not have placed Lady Teazle out of ear-shot to have saved their ears from the pillory.'

NOTES

Richard Cumberland (1733–1811), English dramatist.
 1. Fitzgerald, *The Lives of the Sheridans*, I, 156n.
 2. George Colman (1732–94), English dramatist and manager of the Haymarket Theatre 1777–89.
 3. Fitzgerald, *The Lives of the Sheridans*, I, 155n.
 4. Ibid., p. 156.
 5. Ibid., p. 156.
 6. *Private Correspondence of David Garrick*, II, 283.
 7. Ibid., p. 285.
 8. Ibid., p. 283.
 9. Ibid., p. 284.
 10. Ibid., p. 286.

11. Tom Davies, author of the *Life of Garrick*.
12. *Memoirs of the Life of David Garrick*, II, 274.
13. Ibid., p. 275.
14. *The Cumberland Letters*, p. 176.
15. *Biographia Dramatica*, III, 51.
16. *A Complete History of the Stage*, V, 275.
17. *Memoirs of the Life of David Garrick*, II, 275.
18. W. H. Ireland's *Vortigern* was a historical tragedy appearing at Drury Lane in 1799. It was an imposition, professing to be an original tragedy of Shakespeare found in an old trunk.
19. Sir Walter Scott, 'Prefatory Memoir to Richard Cumberland', in *Novels of Swift, Bage and Cumberland*, p. 41.
20. John Watkins, *Memoirs of the Public and Private Life of R. B. Sheridan, with a Particular Account of His Family and Connexions* (London: Henry Colburn, 1817) I, 239.
21. *Sheridaniana; or Anecdotes of the Life of Richard Brinsley Sheridan, His Table Talk and Bon Mots* (London: Henry Colburn, 1826) p. 67.
22. See Watkins, *Memoirs of Sheridan*, I, 237.
23. Ibid., p. 238.
24. Adolphus, *Life of Bannister*, I, 47.
25. [William Earle], *Sheridan and His Times*, by an Octogenarian, who Stood by His Knee in Youth and Sat at His Table in Manhood (London: J. F. Hope, 1859) I, 95.
26. Sheridan, *The Critic*, I, i.
27. Richard Cumberland, *British Theatre*, p. 18.
28. *The Eccentricities of John Edwin*, II, 307.
29. James Boaden, *Memoirs of the Life of John Philip Kemble* (London: Longman, Hurst, Rees, Orme, Brown and Green, 1825) I, 36. Kelly describes Parsons as Sir Fretful.
30. Leigh Hunt regarded Mathews' Sir Fretful as perfect. The actor was painted in the role by De Wilde.
31. *The Journal of Walter Scott*, I, 79.
32. Scott, 'Prefatory Memoir to Cumberland', in *The Novels of Swift, Bage and Cumberland*. Walter Sichel in his *Sheridan, from New and Original Material* (London: Constable, 1909) thinks Sir Fretful an exact portrait of Cumberland. He notes the erasure in the first draft of the scene, showing that Cumberland was originally treated even more severely.

Extremely Happy*

FANNY BURNEY

The elegance of Mrs Sheridan's beauty is unequalled by any that I ever saw, except Mrs Crewe.¹ I was pleased with her in all respects. She is much more lively and agreeable than I had any idea of finding her; she was very gay and unaffected and totally free from airs of any kind. . . . Mr Sheridan has a fine figure, and a good, though I don't think a handsome, face. He is tall and very upright, and his appearance and address are at once manly and fashionable without the smallest tincture of foppery or modish graces. In short, I like him vastly, and think him every way worthy of his beautiful companion. And let me tell you what I know will give you as much pleasure as it gave me, that, by all I could observe in the course of the evening, and we stayed very late, they are extremely happy in each other: he evidently adores her, and she as evidently idolizes him. The world has by no means done him justice.

NOTES

Frances (Fanny) Burney (1752–1840), English novelist who married General d'Arblay in 1793. She met the Sheridans in 1779, at the time when she was in the full blossom of popularity as the author of *Eveline*, her first and most admirable novel.

    1. Frances Crewe. Sheridan's attachment to her, his 'Amoret', was prolonged and probably serious.

---

* *Diary and Letters of Madame D'Arblay*, ed. C. Barrett (London: Bickers and Son, 1876) I, 182.

At Drury Lane*

MRS SIDDONS

... just as I had finished my toilette, and was pondering with fearfulness my first appearance in the grand fiendish part, comes Mr Sheridan knocking at my door, and insisting, in spite of all my entreaties not to be interrupted at this to me tremendous moment, to be admitted. He would not be denied admittance, for he protested he must speak to me on a circumstance which so deeply concerned my own interest, that it was of the most serious nature. Well, after much squabbling I was compelled to admit him, that I might dismiss him the sooner and compose myself before the play began. But what was my distress and astonishment when I found that he wanted me even at this moment of anxiety and terror to adopt another mode of acting the sleeping scene! He told me that he had heard with the greatest surprise and concern that I meant to act it without holding the candle in my hand; and when I argued the impracticability of washing out that '*damned spot*' that was certainly implied by both her own words and those of her gentlewomen, he insisted, that if I did put the candle out of my hand it would be thought a presumptuous innovation, as Mrs Pritchard had always retained it in hers.[1] My mind, however, was made up, and it was then too late to make me alter it, for I was too agitated to adopt another method. My deference for Mr Sheridan's taste and judgment was, however, so great, that, had he proposed the alteration whilst it was possible for me to change my own plan I should have yielded to his suggestion. ... The scene of course was acted as I had myself conceived it, and the innovation, as Mr Sheridan called it, was received with approbation. Mr Sheridan himself came to me after the play, and most ingenuously congratulated me on my obstinacy.

NOTES

Sheridan never missed a first night at Drury Lane Theatre, and was always interested in the minutiae and technique of acting. Mrs Sarah Siddons (1755–

---

* Percy H. Fitzgerald, *The Kembles: An Account of the Kemble Family, Including the Lives of Mrs Siddons, and Her Brother J. P. Kemble* (London, 1871) I, 241. Editor's title.

1831), English actress, makes his intense interest in the production of *Macbeth* clear in this recollection.

    1. Sheridan was sometimes a stickler for stage conventions, but Mrs Siddons stuck to her point and acted the scene to her own taste.

Meets Fox*

LORD JOHN TOWNSHEND

I made the first dinner-party at which they met; having told Fox that all the notions he might have conceived of Sheridan's talents and genius from the comedy of *The Rivals*, etc. would fall infinitely short of the admiration of his astonishing powers, which I was sure he would entertain at the first interview. The first interview between them . . . I shall never forget. Fox told me, after breaking up from dinner, that he had always thought Hare,[1] after my uncle, Charles Townshend, the wittiest man he ever met with, but that Sheridan surpassed them both infinitely; and Sheridan told me next day that he was quite lost in admiration of Fox, and that it was a puzzle to him to say what he admired most, his commanding superiority of talents and universal knowledge, or his playful fancy, artless manners, and benevolence of heart, which showed itself in every word he uttered.

NOTES

For a decade Sheridan had been dabbling in political journalism, and had also come to know many of the leading politicians of the day at Devonshire House, the bastion of Whiggism presided over by the Duchess of Devonshire. The most important meeting, however, was with Charles James Fox (1749–1806), by now clearly destined to play a leading role in any prospective Whig administration. Lord John Townshend describes their first encounter but does not give it a date.

    1. James Hare, a member of the Whig Party in the House of Commons.

* From Margaret Oliphant, *Sheridan*, English Men of Letters series (London: Macmillan, 1883) p. 120. Editor's title.

In Parliament*

SIR NATHANIEL WRAXALL

Sheridan reappeared in the new House of Commons by Fox's[1] side. He possessed a ductility and versatility of talents which no public man in our time has equalled, and these intellectual endowments were sustained by a suavity of temper that seemed to set at defiance all efforts to ruffle or discompose it. Playing with his irritable or angry antagonist, Sheridan exposed him by sallies of wit or attacked him with classic elegance of satire, performing this arduous task in the face of a crowded assembly without losing for an instant either his presence of mind, his facility of expression or his good humour. He wounded deepest, when he smiled, and convulsed his hearers with laughter while the object of his ridicule or animadversion was twisting under the lash. Pitt[2] and Dundas,[3] who presented the fairest marks for his attack, found by experience that, though they might repel, they could not confound, still less could they silence or vanquish him. In every attempt that they made, by introducing personalities or illiberal reflexions on his private life or dramatic occupations, to disconcert him, he turned their weapons on themselves.

Nor did he, while thus chastising his adversary, alter a muscle of his own countenance which, as well as his gestures, seemed to participate and display the unalterable serenity of his intellectual formation. Rarely did he elevate his voice, and never except in subservience to the dictates of his judgement, with the view to produce a corresponding effect on his audience. Yet he was always heard, generally listened to with eagerness, and could obtain a hearing at almost any hour. Burke,[4] who wanted Sheridan's nice tact and his amenity of manner, was continually coughed down, and on those occasions he lost his temper. Even Fox often tired the House by the repetitions which he introduced into his speeches. Sheridan never abused their patience. Whenever he rose, they anticipated a rich repast of wit without acrimony, seasoned by allusions and citations the most delicate, yet obvious in their application.

At this period of his life, when he was not more than thirty-three years of age, his countenance and features had in them something peculiarly pleasing, indicative at once of intellect, humour and gaiety.

---

* *The Historical and Posthumous Memoirs of Sir N. W. Wraxall*, ed. H. B. Wheatley (London: Bickers and Sons, 1884) III, 367–8.

All these characteristics played about his lips when speaking, and operated with inconceivable attraction; for they anticipated, as it were, to the eye, the effect produced by his oratory on the ear, thus opening for him a sure way to the heart of the understanding. Even the tones of his voice, which were singularly mellifluous, aided the general effect of his eloquence; nor was it accompanied by Burke's unpleasant Irish accent. Pitt's enunciation was unquestionably more imposing, dignified and sonorous. Fox displayed more argument as well as vehemence; Burke possessed more fancy and enthusiasim; but Sheridan won his way by a sort of fascination.

NOTES

In 1780, the second phase of Sheridan's career began when he was elected to Parliament as the member for Stafford. He was again returned by his constituents at the general election of 1784. Wraxall (1751–1831), a member of the same Parliament, a political opponent, and especially incensed against anyone who had taken an active part in the measures of the Coalition Ministry, draws this picture of Sheridan early in his political career.
  1. Charles James Fox (1749–1806), English statesman and orator.
  2. William Pitt (1759–1806), English statesman and Prime Minister.
  3. Henry Dundas, Viscount Melville (1742–1811), British statesman.
  4. Edmund Burke (1729–97), British statesman and orator.

The Orator*

SIR GILBERT ELLIOT

This last night, though the House was up soon after one . . ., I have not slept *one wink*. Nothing whatever was the matter with me, except the impression of what had been passing still vibrating on my brain. . . . Sheridan opened his charge, and spoke exactly five hours and a half, with such fluency and rapidity that I think his speech could not be read in double the time. You may imagine the quantity of matter it contained. It was by many degrees the most excellent and astonishing performance I ever heard, and surpasses all I ever imagined possible in eloquence and ability. This is the *universal* sense of all who heard it.

* From Sir Gilbert Elliot, *Life and Letters* (London: Longman, 1874). Editor's title.

You will conceive how admirable it was when I tell you that he surpassed, I think, Pitt, Fox, and even Burke, in his finest and most brilliant orations. . . . It is impossible to describe the feelings he excited. The *bone* rose repeatedly in my throat, and tears in my eyes – not of grief, but merely of strongly excited sensibility. . . . The conclusion, in which the whole force of the case was collected, and where his whole powers were employed to their utmost stretch, and indeed his own feelings wound to the utmost pitch, worked the House into such a paroxysm of passionate enthusiasm on the subject, and of admiration for him, that the moment he sat down there was a universal shout, nay, even clapping, for half-a-second; every man was on the floor, and all his friends throwing themselves on his neck in raptures of joy and exultation. . . . All the Ministry and all the friends of Hastings were struck absolutely dumb, and sat confounded, not knowing how, nor daring to meet the impression made on the audience; and after Burgess had talked absolute nonsense for an hour in favour of Hastings, they recollected themselves enough to move for an adjournment till to-day.

NOTE

The problem of India was tackled by the Whigs in 1787 by attacking the great governor Warren Hastings (1732–1818), who had come home with a reputation for efficiency and ruthlessness. Sheridan spoke all through the night of 7 February 1787 in the Commons, on the motion to impeach Hastings before the Lords, and carried the House with him. The speech Sheridan delivered is considered one of the great speeches in the history of Parliament. Owing to the inadequacies of journalism at the time, all that remains is a skeleton. Burke, Fox and Pitt paid the speech effusive tribute, and Sir Gilbert Elliot (1751–1814), the English diplomat and a future Governor-General of Bengal, gave this account of it in a letter to his wife the next day.

Witchcraft*

SIR HORACE WALPOLE

One heard everybody in the streets raving on the wonders of that speech; for my part I cannot believe it was so supernatural as they

---

* From *Letters Addressed to the Countess of Ossory, from the Year 1769 to 1797*, ed. R. V. Smith (London: Richard Bentley, 1848) vol. 2, pp. 298–9. Editor's title.

say – do you believe it was, Madam? . . . How should such a fellow as Sheridan, who has no diamonds to bestow, fascinate all the world? – Yet witchcraft, no doubt, there has been, for when did simple eloquence ever convince a majority? Mr Pitt and 174 other persons found Mr Hastings guilty last night. . . . Well, at least there is a new crime, sorcery, to charge on the opposition!

NOTE

In this letter to the Countess of Ossory, Sir Horace Walpole (1717–97), English man of letters, commented on accounts of Sheridan's speech.

Pride Filled My Heart*

ELIZABETH SHERIDAN
(Sheridan's sister)

Just as I received your letter yesterday, I was setting out for the Trial[1] with Mrs Crewe and Mrs Dixon. I was fortunate in my day, as I heard all the principal speakers – Mr Burke I admired the least – Mr Fox very much indeed. The subject in itself was not particularly interesting, as the debate turned merely on a point of law, but the earnestness of his manner and the amazing precision with which he conveys his ideas is truly delightful. And last, not least, I heard my brother! I cannot express to you the sensation of pleasure and pride that filled my heart at the moment he rose. Had I never seen him or heard his name before, I should have conceived him the first man among them at once. There is a dignity and grace in his countenance and deportment, very striking – at the same time that one cannot trace the smallest degree of conscious superiority in his manner. His voice, too, appeared to me extremely fine. The speech itself was not much calculated to display the talents of an orator, as of course it related only to dry matter. You may suppose I am not so lavish of praises before indifferent persons, but I am sure you will acquit me of partiality in what I have said. When they left the Hall we walked about some time, and were joined by several of the managers – among the rest by Mr Burke, whom we set down at his own house. They seem now to have better hopes of the

* From Moore, *Memoirs of Sheridan*, II, 41–2. Editor's title.

business than they have had for some time; as the point urged with so much force and apparent success relates to very material evidence which the Lords have refused to hear, but which, once produced, must prove strongly against Mr Hastings; and, from what passed yesterday, they think their Lordships must yield. – We sat in the King's box. . . .

NOTES

Sheridan's sister Elizabeth (Betsy) was visiting her brother in London when she wrote the above accounts in a letter to her sister Alicia in Dublin. Elizabeth Sheridan married Henry Lefanu in 1789. (The two Elizabeth Sheridans, his sister and his first wife, were usually distinguished by different diminutives, Betsy and Eliza.)

1. The trial of Warren Hastings began in Westminster Hall in June 1788. Sheridan's dazzling performance on 7 February 1787 in the Commons had now to be repeated in a different form.

Dick's Triumph*

ELIZABETH SHERIDAN
(Sheridan's wife)

I have delayed writing till I could gratify myself and you by sending you the news of our dear Dick's triumph! – of our triumph, I may call it; for, surely, no one in the slightest degree connected with him, but must feel proud and happy. It is impossible, my dear woman, to convey to you the delight, the astonishment, the adoration, he has excited in the breasts of every class of people! Even party prejudice has been overcome by a display of genius, eloquence and goodness which no one with anything like a heart about them, could have listened to, without being the wiser and the better for the rest of their lives. What must *my* feelings be! – you can only imagine. To tell you the truth, it is with some difficulty that I can 'let down my mind', as Mr Burke said afterwards, to talk or think on any other subject. But pleasure, too exquisite, becomes pain, and I am at this moment suffering for the delightful anxieties of last week. . . . I hope by next week we shall be quietly settled in the country, and suffered to *repose*, in every sense of

* From Rae, *Sheridan: A Biography*, II, 74. Editor's title.

the word; for indeed we have both of us been in a constant state of agitation, of one kind or another, for some time back.

NOTE

Sheridan's wife Elizabeth (Eliza) wrote this letter to her sister-in-law Alicia in Dublin.

Tumult of Applause*

For five hours and a half Mr Sheridan commanded the universal interest and admiration of the house (which from the expectation of the day was uncommonly crowded) by an oration of almost unexampled excellence, uniting the most convincing closeness and accuracy of argument with the most luminous precision and perspicuity of language, and alternately giving form and energy to truth by solid and substantial reasoning; and enlightening the most extensive and involved subjects with the purest clearness of logic and the brightest splendours of rhetoric. Every prejudice, every prepossession, was gradually overcome by the force of this extraordinary combination of keen but liberal discrimination; of brilliant yet argumentative wit. So fascinated were the auditors by his eloquence that when Mr Sheridan sat down the whole house – the members, peers, and strangers – involuntarily joined in a tumult of applause, and adopted a mode of expressing their admiration, new and irregular in the house, by loudly and repeatedly clapping with their hands. Mr Burke declared it to be the most astonishing effort of eloquence, argument, and wit united of which there was any record or tradition. Mr Fox said, 'All that he had ever heard – all that he had ever read – when compared with it dwindled into nothing, and vanished like vapour before the sun.' Mr Pitt acknowledged that it surpassed all the eloquence of ancient or of modern times, and possessed everything that genius or art could furnish to agitate and control the human mind. The effects it produced were

---

* *The Speeches of the Right Honourable Richard Brinsley Sheridan with a Sketch of His Life.* Edited by a Constitutional Friend [Sir John Phillipart?] (London: P. Martin, 1816). Editor's title.

proportioned to its merits. After a considerable suspension of the debate, one of the friends of Mr Hastings – Mr Burgess[1] – with some difficulty obtained for a short time a hearing; but, finding the house too strongly affected by what they had heard to listen to him with favour, sat down again. Several members confessed they had come down strongly prepossessed in favour of the person accused, and imagined nothing less than a miracle could have wrought so entire a revolution in their sentiments. Others declared that though they could not resist the conviction that flashed upon their minds, yet they wished to have leave to cool before they were called upon to vote; and though they were persuaded it would require another miracle to produce another change in their opinions, yet for the sake of decorum they thought it proper that the debate should be adjourned. Mr Fox and Mr A. Taylor strongly opposed this proposition, contending that it was not less absurd than unparliamentary to defer coming to a vote for no other reason that had been alleged than because members were too firmly convinced; but Mr Pitt concurring with the opinions of the former, the debate was adjourned.

NOTES

This account, corroborated by many witnesses, is taken from the summary given at the head of the extracts from Sheridan's oration in the collection of his speeches.

1. John Burgess, attorney.

Done with the Stage*

CHARLES DIBDIN

Mr Sheridan can write in any style, and to any degree of perfection he pleases, but his public writing, like his public speaking is more *catching* than *captivating*; it dazzles, but does not *impress* – it charms but does not *convince*. In short, as that gentleman's aim is popularity, he does everything for the moment, and it is a question, after he has sunk into ease and independence, from his natural indolence of mind, whether

* From *The Reminiscences of Thomas Dibdin* (London: Henry Colburn, 1827). Editor's title.

he will ever again be known but by a few eminent trifles.... Mr Sheridan having most probably done with the stage, as an author, it is but fair to examine how far, in that capacity, he has been an acquisition to the public; and when we consider that he has deprived the world of the best singer,[1] beyond all comparison, that we have ever heard, it is very doubtful whether what he has given be adequate to what he has taken away...

NOTES

It was the musical fame of his wife that had first offered Sheridan a passport to the drawing-rooms of the aristocracy, as his enemies often chose to remind him. The hostile Charles Dibdin (1745–1814), dramatist and musician, had this to say.

1. When Sheridan married Elizabeth Linley in 1773, she could earn large sums by her singing. To the general surprise, however, Sheridan firmly refused to allow her to do this. Sheridan's objection was to allowing his wife to appear on a public stage to be stared at and applauded by anyone who cared to pay the price of a seat; and it was on this ground that Dr Samuel Johnson heartily approved of his decision.

By His Father's Side*

DR DANIEL JARVIS

On the 10th of August, 1788, I was first called on to visit Mr Sheridan, who was then fast declining at his lodgings in this place, where he was in the care of his daughter.[1] On the next day Mr R. B. Sheridan arrived here from town, having brought with him Dr Morris, of Parliament Street. I was in the bedroom with Mr Sheridan when the son arrived, and witnessed an interview in which the father showed himself to be strongly impressed by his son's attention, saying with considerable emotion, 'Oh Dick, I give you a great deal of trouble!' and seeming to imply by his manner, that his son had been less to blame than himself, for any previous want of cordiality between them.

On my making my last call for the evening, Mr R. B. Sheridan, with delicacy, but much earnestness, expressed his fear that the nurse in

* From Moore, *Memoirs of Sheridan*, II, 51–2. Editor's title.

attendance on his father, might not be so competent as myself to the requisite attentions, and his hope that I would consent to remain in the room for a few of the first hours of the night; as he himself, having been travelling the preceding night, required some short repose. I complied with his request, and remained at the father's bed-side till relieved by the son, about three o'clock in the morning: – he then insisted on taking my place. From this time he never quitted the house till his father's death; on the day after which he wrote me a letter, now before me, of which the annexed is an exact copy:

Friday Morning.
Sir,
I wished to see you this morning before I went, to thank you for your attention and trouble. You will be so good to give the account to Mr Thompson,[2] who will settle it; and I must further beg your acceptance of the inclosed from myself.
I am, Sir,
Your obedient Servant,
R. B. Sheridan.

I have explained to Dr Morris (who has informed me that you will recommend a proper person), that it is my desire to have the hearse, and the manner of coming to town, as respectful as possible.

The inclosure, referred to in this letter, was a bank-note of ten pounds – a most liberal remuneration. Mr R. B. Sheridan left Margate, intending that his father should be buried in London; but he there ascertained that it had been his father's expressed wish that he should be buried in the parish next to that in which he should happen to die. He then, consequently, returned to Margate, accompanied by his brother-in-law, Mr Tickell, with whom and Mr Thompson and myself, he followed his father's remains to the burial-place, which was not in Margate church-yard, but in the north aisle of the church of St Peter's.

NOTES

In the summer of 1788, Sheridan's father became ill and was recommended to try the air of Lisbon for his health. But the rapid increase of his malady prevented him from proceeding farther than Margate, where he died on 14 August, attended in his last moments by his son Richard Brinsley, while the paragon son Charles Francis stayed in Ireland. This account was written by

Dr Daniel Jarvis, who attended him, at the request of Thomas Moore, Sheridan's biographer.
1. Elizabeth (Betsy) Sheridan.
2. Servant of Thomas Sheridan.

My Brother's Kindness*

ELIZABETH SHERIDAN
(Sheridan's sister)

My Dear Love,

Though you have ever been uppermost in my thoughts, yet it has not been in my power to write since the few lines I sent from Margate. I hope this will find you, in some degree, recovered from the shock you must have experienced from the late melancholy event. I trust to your own piety and the tenderness of your worthy husband,[1] for procuring you such a degree of calmness of mind as may secure your health from injury. In the midst of what I have suffered I have been thankful that you did not share a scene of distress which you could not have relieved. I have supported myself, but I am sure, had we been together, we should have suffered more.

With regard to my brother's kindness, I can scarcely express to you how great it has been. He saw my father while he was still sensible, and never quitted him till the awful moment was past – I will not now dwell on particulars. My mind is not sufficiently recovered to enter on the subject, and you could only be distressed by it. He returns soon to Margate to pay the last duties in the manner desired by my father. His feelings have been severely tried, and earnestly I pray he may not suffer from that cause, or from the fatigue he has endured. His tenderness to me I never can forget. I had so little claim on him, that I still feel a degree of surprise mixed with my gratitude. Mrs Sheridan's reception of me was truly affectionate.[2] They leave me to myself now as much as I please, as I had gone through so much fatigue of body and mind that I require some rest. I have not, as you may suppose, looked much beyond the present hour, but I begin to be more composed. I could now enjoy your society, and I wish for it hourly. I should think I may hope to see you sooner in England than you had intended; but you will write to me very soon, and let me know everything that

* *Betsy Sheridan's Journal: Letters from Sheridan's Sister 1784–1786 and 1788–1790*, ed. William LeFanu (London: Eyre and Spottiswoode, 1960) pp. 116–17. Editor's title.

concerns you. I know not whether you will feel like me a melancholy pleasure in the reflection that my father received the last kind offices from my brother Richard, whose conduct on this occasion must convince every one of the goodness of his heart and the truth of his filial affection. One more reflection of consolation is, that nothing was omitted that could have prolonged his life or eased his latter hours. God bless and preserve you, my dear love. I shall soon write more to you, but shall for a short time suspend my journal, as still too many painful thoughts will crowd upon me to suffer me to regain such a frame of mind as I should wish when I write to you.
    Ever affectionately your
E. Sheridan.

NOTES

Immediately on the death of their father, Sheridan removed his sister Elizabeth (Betsy) to Deepdene – a seat of the Duke of Norfolk in Surrey, which His Grace had lately lent him – and then returned, himself, to Margate, to pay the last tribute to his father's remains. This letter, dated 18 August 1788, is addressed to Elizabeth's sister Alicia in Dublin.
  1. Joseph Lefanu, whom Alicia Sheridan married in 1781.
  2. After Thomas Sheridan died, Sheridan and his wife welcomed Elizabeth at first in the country and later in Bruton Street. She lived with them till her marriage to Henry Lefanu nearly a year later.

The Excessive Drinker*

ELIZABETH SHERIDAN
(Sheridan's wife)

I see you are ever so affronted with me, but upon my life without the least cause. I have never had one *cross* feel towards you since you left Crewe,[1] but I must say whatever is in my mind to say on all subjects, you know, and when you tell me how vexed and grieved you was at not being able to speak that Monday, on account of your making yourself so ill on Sunday, would you have me say drinking to that excess is *not an abominable habit*? And where I see *idletons* as Jack

---

* From Rae, *Sheridan: A Biography*, II, 128–9. Editor's title.

Townshend can overcome all your good, and strong resolutions, mustn't I think that London and its inhabitants and their ways *do* alter people whether they will or no?

These are the expressions you seem to take so ill, and upon my life I don't see how I can retract them, only that I protest I never had an idea of being cross or giving you a moment's vexation by them; for indeed, my soul, you have been the dear good one ever since you left me, and so far from thinking, or saying, you neglected me, I have often wondered at your attention, and particularly, knowing how much you have to do; but yet, I should be very sorry if you were less so, and when you have missed your days [for writing], I have been disappointed and grieved, and of course my letters must have shown it, but I'll be hanged if they were cross, or if I have ever felt the least so since the first week. Your letters, my heart, are all the comfort and amusement I have. I have lost all pleasure in cribbage, for Mr C[rewe] beats me so constantly and unmercifully, that it is quite disgusting. . . .

God love thee as well as I do and you will sit upon the finest cloud in Heaven and be better than all his cherubims. So good-night.[2]

NOTES

By April 1790, Elizabeth (Eliza) sometimes grieved over Sheridan for giving way to drink, as this letter to him shows.

1. Crewe Hall, Cheshire, home of Mrs (later Lady) Crewe, the dedicatee of *The School for Scandal*. The decade was not far advanced when Elizabeth had also to face the fact that her husband was unfaithful to her. Acclimatised by now to the ways of the aristocratic world, she seems to have been distressed but not shocked. Indeed, while Sheridan was engaged in his affair with Mrs Crewe, Elizabeth remained on very good terms with her.

2. The letter was continued on the following day, when the receipt of one is acknowledged with thanks for Sheridan's goodness and punctuality.

My Dearest Hetty*

ELIZABETH SHERIDAN
(Sheridan's wife)

Crew Hall, Jan. 10th [1791].

* 'Some Unpublished Letters of Mrs Sheridan to Mrs Canning', ed. Michael T. H. Sadleir as Appendix III of Sadleir, *The Political Career of Richard Brinsley Sheridan* (The Stanhope Essay for 1912) (Oxford: B. H. Blackwell, 1912) pp. 81–5. Editor's title.

My dearest Hetty will perhaps think it unkind that I have been so long at this seat of hospitable jollity without giving her some accounts of our proceeding. . . . I cannot bear you shd think I neglect you, and therefore I have determined to tell you the real Cause of my silence. It is impossible in a Letter to detail the thousand Causes I have for Vexation, but do not let it make you too unhappy if you hear that S. and I shall most probably come to an amicable separation when I return to town. We have been sometime separated *in fact* as man and wife. The World, my dear Hetty, is a bad one, and we are both Victims of its Seductions. S. has involved himself by his Gallantries and cannot retreat. The Duplicity of his Conduct to me has hurt me more than anything else, and I confess to you that my Heart is entirely alienated from him, and I see no prospect of Happiness for either of us but in the Proposal I have made him of Parting. Do not suppose that I will ever do anything to disgrace myself or my family. The D. of C[larence] (tho' I own to you I am not indifferent to his devoted Attachment for me, and have thought more favourably of him still since I have had reason to make comparisons between his Conduct and S's) has nothing to do with this determination, nor does he even guess my intention. You may rely on the propriety of my Conduct in regard to him for many sakes, but I will in future live by myself and to my own tastes.

Friday morn. [1791.]

My dearest Hetty,

. . . You will not be sorry to hear that I have at last consented to pass an Act of Oblivion over all S's Vagaries, and that we are at present on very comfortable terms. I don't know in my life that ever I passed so many miserable Hours as I did for the last weeks I was at Crewe. S. had so completely involved himself with Lady D——n [Duncannon][1] that a suit was actually commenced against them in Doctors Commons, and if the D. of Devon had not come over to England and exerted his influence with Ld D[uncannon] by this time S. wd have been an object of Ridicule and Abuse to all the World. However, thank God the Business is hush'd up. I believe principally on old Ld Bessborough's account and she is going abroad very soon, I believe to her Sister. You will imagine this affair gave me no little uneasiness, but can you believe it possible that at the very time when S. was pleading for forgiveness from me on this account, before it was certain that it wd be hush'd up, at the moment almost in wh he was swearing and imprecating all sorts of Curses on himself on me and his Child, if ever he was led away by any Motive to be false to me again, he threw the whole Family at Crewe into Confusion and Distress, by playing the fool with Miss Fd[Ford] (little Emma's governess) and contriving so awkwardly too, as to be discovered by the whole House, locked up with her in a Bed Chamber in an unfrequented part of the House. I confess to you, my dear Hetty, that this last instance of his duplicity, the apparent total want of all feeling for me, of all sense of Honour, Delicacy, Propriety, considering the *Person*, the *Place*, and the *Time* when he indulged so unwarrantable an inclination, provok'd me so much beyond all bounds, that I am confident had the D. of C. been six and thirty instead of six and twenty, I should have run away with him directly, tho' most probably I shd have hung myself a Week afterwards. But fortunately the distance between us gave time for reflection, and I only determined to live no longer with S. This was the time when I wrote you the letter wh I daresay alarmed you. I kept my Resolution a great while and even parted with S. quite unreconciled to him. . . . But I don't know how it is. I have been talked over by Mrs B[?ouverie] Ch. Fox and S. himself has been so terribly frightened and affected by my Behaviour, that at last I have received him once more into favour, tho', I own to you I have lost all Confidence in his professions and promises. However for those dear Creatures who are always brought as strong arguments against any rash step, I shall endeavour if possible to keep him steady to his good Resolutions.

[The letter goes on to describe the importunate passion of the Duke of Clarence, Mrs Sheridan's strong inclination to yield to his desires, her final decision to throw off his attentions, the efforts of the Prince of Wales to control his brother, and ends with an expression of thankfulness that the troubles are now over.]

C[rewe] H[ouse], Jan. 27th [1791.]

My dearest Hetty,

I write a few lines to you before I leave Crewe, as I think it will give you pleasure to hear that Matters are in some sort made up between S. and me. . . . S's Sorrow . . . for having made me so unhappy, and for having exposed me so often to Temptations and Dangers (wh God knows how I have hitherto escaped) has made some impression on my Heart, and in short I have been softened into forgiveness, and may yet look forward to domestic Happiness sometime or other, tho' I am convinced, notwithstanding Oaths and Professions, not yet for many Years. We are both now descending the Hill pretty fast, and tho' we take different paths, perhaps we shall meet at the Bottom at last, and then our Wanderings and Deviations may serve for Moralising in our Chimney Corner some twenty years hence.

[The letter concludes with a further description of the persecutions of the Duke of Clarence.]

[? May 27, 1792.]

I have and do most solemnly promise my dear friend Mrs S. to protect and guard her poor child thro' Life and to do my utmost to breed her up like my own. That is saying enough – .

I here solemnly promise my dear Betsy[2] never to interfere on any account with Mrs C[anning] in the education or in any other way of my poor child. I cannot write all I wish but he knows my Heart. Swear or I shall not die in peace – .

[The above lines were written by Mrs Sheridan on her deathbed. The handwriting is wavering, the composition confused; the writer is sinking fast. The first paragraph was to be signed by Mrs Canning, to whom the child was to be confided. The second by Sheridan himself. It will be noticed that in the last two sentences of the second paragraph Mrs Sheridan's thoughts wander, and she seems to address Sheridan personally.]

NOTES

Mrs Stratford Canning, *née* Patrick, was Elizabeth Sheridan's dearest friend in the later years of her life. Tom Sheridan (Sheridan's son) and George Canning were schoolfriends. Elizabeth turned to Mrs Canning for peace and relief from the bustle of a London life she hated. (Editorial matter in square brackets is Sadleir's.)

1. [Lady Duncannon, afterwards Lady Bessborough, was the sister of the Duchess of Devonshire.]
2. 'Betsy' is Sheridan's younger sister Elizabeth (1758–1837), who married Henry Lefanu in 1789. 'The name Elizabeth Sheridan was shared by Sheridan's sister and his wife between 1773 and 1789. Mrs R. B. Sheridan, however, was usually called Eliza, though her own sister Mary Tickell called them both Betsy, and Eliza sometimes used this name herself' – *Betsy Sheridan's Journal: Letters from Sheridan's Sister*, ed. William Lefanu (London: Eyre and Spottiswoode, 1960) xii.

Fading in Sickness*

RICHARD BRINSLEY SHERIDAN

Night, Silence, Solitude, and the Sea combined will unhinge the cheerfulness of anyone where there has been length of Life enough to bring regret in reflecting on many past scenes, and to offer slender hope in anticipating the future. . . . How many years have passed since on these unreasoning, restless waters, which this night I have been gazing at and listening to; I bore poor E., who is now so near me fading in sickness, from all her natural attachments and affections. . . . What has the interval of my Life been, and what is left me but misery from Memory and a horror of Reflexion?

I stopt yesterday evening as we came over King's Down . . . and went to the spot where my life was strangely saved once. . . .[1] What an interval has passed since, and scarce one promise that I then made to my own soul have I attempted to fulfil. . . . My nerves are shook to pieces. The irregularity of all my Life and pursuits, the restless, contriving temper with which I have persevered in wrong Pursuits and Passions makes . . . reflexion worse to me than even to those who have acted worse. . . .

NOTES

During the last weeks of his wife's sickness, Sheridan kept up his spirits heroically before her; but sorrow sat on his countenance, and in his journal letter to Georgiana and her sister Lady Duncannon (later Lady Bessborough) the real man became articulate in his misery.

1. During a duel with Captain Thomas Mathews in 1772.

---

* From Walter Sichel, *Sheridan, from New and Original Material* (London: Constable, 1909) II 435, 437. Editor's title.

An Agonising Scene*

MRS STRATFORD CANNING

19 July, 1792.

Our dear departed friend kept her bed only two days, and seemed to suffer less during that interval than for some time before. She was perfectly in her senses to the last moment, and talked with the greatest composure of her approaching dissolution; assuring us all that she had the most perfect confidence in the mercies of an all-powerful and merciful Being, from whom alone she could have derived the inward comfort and support she felt at that awful moment! She said, she had no fear of death, and that all her concern arose from the thoughts of leaving so many dear and tender ties, and of what they would suffer from her loss. Her own family were at Bath, and had spent one day with her, when she was tolerably well. Your poor brother now thought it proper to send for them, and to flatter them no longer. They immediately came; – it was the morning before she died. They were introduced one at a time at her bed-side, and were prepared as much as possible for this sad scene. The women bore it very well, but all our feelings were awakened for her poor father. The interview between him and the dear angel was afflicting and heart-breaking to the greatest degree imaginable. I was afraid she would have sunk under the cruel agitation: – she said it was indeed too much for her. She gave some kind injunction to each of them, and said everything she could to comfort them under this severe trial. They then parted, in the hope of seeing her again in the evening, but they never saw her more! Mr Sheridan and I sat up all that night with her – indeed he had done so for several nights before, and never left her one moment that could be avoided. About four o'clock in the morning we perceived an alarming change, and sent for her physician.[1] She said to him, 'If you can relieve me, do it quickly; – if not do not let me struggle, but give me some laudanum.' His answer was, 'Then I will give you some laudanum.' She desired to see Tom[2] and Betty Tickell[3] before she took it, of whom she took a most affecting leave! Your brother behaved most wonderfully, though his heart was breaking; and at times his feelings were so violent, that I feared he would have been quite ungovernable at the last. Yet he summoned up courage to kneel by the bed-side, till he felt the last

---

* From Moore, *Memoirs of Sheridan*, II, 134–7. Editor's title.

pulse of expiring excellence, and then withdrew. She died at five o'clock in the morning, 28th of June.

I hope, my dear Mrs Lefanu, you will excuse my dwelling on this most agonising scene. I have a melancholy pleasure in so doing, and fancy it will not be disagreeable to you to hear all the particulars of an event so interesting, so afflicting, to all who knew the beloved creature! For my part, I never beheld such a scene – never suffered such a conflict – much as I have suffered on my own account. While I live, the remembrance of it and the dear lost object can never be effaced from my mind.

We remained ten days after the event took place at Bristol; and on the 7th instant Mr Sheridan and Tom, accompanied by all her family (except Mrs Linley),[4] Mr and Mrs Leigh,[5] Betty Tickell and myself, attended the dear remains[6] to Wells, where we saw her laid beside her beloved sister in the Cathedral. The choir attended; and there was such a concourse of people of all sorts assembled on the occasion that we could hardly move along. Mr Leigh read the service in a most affecting manner. Indeed, the whole scene, as you may easily imagine, was awful and affecting to a very great degree. Though the crowd certainly interrupted the solemnity very much, and, perhaps, happily for us abated somewhat of our feelings, which, had we been less observed, would not have been so easily kept down.

The day after the sad scene was closed we separated, your brother choosing to be left by himself with Tom for a day or two. He afterwards joined us at Bath, where we spent a few days with our friends, the Leighs. Last Saturday we took leave of them, and on Sunday we arrived at Isleworth, where with much regret, I left your brother to his own melancholy reflections, with no other companions but his two children, in whom he seems at present entirely wrapped up. He suffered a great deal in returning the same road, and was most dreadfully agitated on his arrival at Isleworth. His grief is deep and sincere, and I am sure will be lasting. He is in very good spirits, and at times is even cheerful, but the moment he is left alone he feels all the anguish of sorrow and regret. The dear little girl[7] is the greatest comfort to him: – he cannot bear to be a moment without her. She thrives amazingly, and is indeed a charming little creature. Tom behaves with constant and tender attention to his father – he laments his dear mother sincerely, and at the time was violently affected; – but, at his age, the impressions of grief are not lasting; and his mind is naturally too lively and cheerful to dwell long on melancholy objects. He is in all respects truly amiable, and in many respects so like his dear, charming mother, that I am sure he will be ever dear to my heart. I expect to have the pleasure of seeing Mr Sheridan again next week, when I hope to find him more composed than when I took leave of him last Sunday.

NOTES

In June 1792, the health of Sheridan's wife Elizabeth deteriorated, and her family came from Bath to see her. Mrs Stratford Canning, a close friend, wrote the details in a letter to Sheridan's sister Alicia (Mrs Joseph Lefanu) in Dublin.
   1. Dr Bain.
   2. Elizabeth's only son, who was born on 17 November 1775.
   3. Elizabeth's niece, whom Elizabeth had adopted after her sister died.
   4. Mary Linley (1729–1820), Elizabeth's mother.
   5. The Revd Mr Leigh and his wife, who were the Sheridans' friends.
   6. 'The following striking reflection, which I have found upon a scrap of paper, in Sheridan's handwriting, was suggested, no doubt, by his feelings on this occasion: "The loss of the breath from a beloved object, long suffering in pain and certainly to die, is not so great a privation as the last loss of her beautiful remains, if they remain so. The victory of the Grave is sharper than the Sting of Death"' Moore, *Memoirs of Sheridan*, II, 136.
   7. Elizabeth's baby Mary, who was born on 30 March 1792.

Tom's Tutor*

WILLIAM SMYTH

I had myself to cast about and consider what effort I could make for my own support, and the support of those who now wanted assistance; no strong exertion was possible, my eyes had been long weakened, there was a nervous affection in the retina; I had thus been prevented from going into any active profession; I could not read more than two or three hours in the day, and not at all at night; I had therefore no other chance but to go tutor into some family, where such services and superintendence, as in that state I could render, might be worth some pecuniary recompense. I therefore wrote, right and left, to my college and other friends, informing them of my wishes, – among the rest, to Mr Edward Morris, with whom I had spent many happy hours while we were fellow-students at Peter-House; and of whose attachment and zeal to serve me I had no doubt. Morris, on his leaving college, had been smit with a passion for the drama; had been guilty of writing a farce, and afterwards a comedy, that was unsuccessful; but had thus been introduced to the acquaintance of Sheridan. The result was, that I received from him a letter, to state that Sheridan's son had been

---

* William Smyth, *Memoir of Mr Sheridan* (Leeds: J. Cross, 1840) pp. 11–20. Editor's title.

brought away from Dr Parr, who could do nothing for him; that he was running wild at Sheridan's seat at Isleworth; the poor mother dead, and the father never there; and that a tutor was wanted for him. The only disagreeable part of this business, said Morris, is this, that Sheridan, though disposed, he assures me, to give every credit to my recommendation, is unwilling to engage with any gentleman whom he has never seen; and, therefore, all that can be done is, that you should come up to town, under pretence of seeing me and other business, and I will bring you together.

This was a bitter pill. Unaccustomed to misfortune, and with all the childish delicacy of one who had 'slept with soft content upon his pillow', I recoiled from the thought of going two hundred miles, to be looked at, and perhaps rejected as an article not worth the purchase. I had heard, too, much of Mr Sheridan's genius, and was sufficiently enamoured of it; but I had heard little of his means or his punctuality as a paymaster. The situation of my family did not admit of any irregularity in this point; and taking into my account the uncivilised state of my pupil's mind, as it might fairly be supposed, the connection appeared to me neither promising nor prudent.

I consulted my confidential friends, who told me that Sheridan, whatever might become of others, would take care to pay *me*; and one of them expatiated on the pleasure and the advantage that I could not but derive, from getting within the inside, as he called it, of such a being as Sheridan.

This part of his discourse 'with greedy ear did I devour'; and as my other friends agreed tolerably well with each other on the point, I took my place in the first stage-coach I could find, and proceeded to London.

I saw Morris — the dinner was arranged – and I was to meet Sheridan and his friend Richardson[1] at seven. I passed the day miserably, but the hour at length arrived.

Richardson was a person of truly amiable disposition, had a great taste for letters, was conversant with the world, and distinguished, even among the Whigs at Brooks's,[2] for the superior powers of his conversation. He had been originally at St John's, and left it to take his chance in the metropolis, and live by his wits, much after the manner of Sheridan himself, of whom he became the bosom friend.

Such a man had no difficulty in making me comfortable and setting me at ease, however awkward my situation. But an hour had now passed, and no Sheridan appeared. Another hour, and Richardson then voted dinner, and made the best apologies he could for Sheridan's characteristic but incorrigible fault; which, it seems, was that of never being punctual; be the engagement what it might. This was not very pleasing intelligence to me; but Richardson and Morris were both very kind; and, though evidently distressed and angry with Sheridan for his remissness, exerted themselves, with some success, to prevent *me* from being so too.

At last a note came to Morris, dated House of Commons, from Sheridan, that he could not possibly get away – that he lamented extremely that he could not have the pleasure of meeting us at dinner – and that he should be most happy to receive us all at the St Albans at twelve, to eat a little supper with him.

This made amends for every thing, and I passed the next two hours very agreeably.

It was then time to go to the tavern, as appointed; but alas! when we enquired at the bar, no tidings could be heard of Mr Sheridan. Any supper ordered? No. Any message? No. Any note? No. – No, no, was the answer to every question that either poor Morris or Richardson could devise. So, as it was a delicious, soft, moonlight night, in the middle of June,[3] we occupied ourselves as we could, traversing Pall-Mall, reciting to each other favourite passages from different authors, now and then interrupted with a word or two from Richardson on the unfortunate habits of his friend Sheridan, and a forlorn sort of call at the bar of the St Albans, to enquire after him and the supper, – the tavern at last seemed to grow weary of us, and we of ourselves. It was now nearly two in the morning; the very moon appeared to be moving off; and I began a course of short speeches to put an end to the business; to express my gratitude for the attentions I had received – the happiness I should have felt in being introduced to so distinguished a man as Mr Sheridan – that I was sorry all such hopes were now at an end – that I had business at Liverpool that admitted of no delay – and that I should go down by the mail the next night.

The mortification and rage of both Morris and Richardson were very visible. 'On any other occasion,' I overheard Richardson say, 'I could have pardoned all this.' Morris followed me, to beg I would not leave town till he had seen me – that he should go to Sheridan in the morning. I begged him not to take the trouble – that I could have no chance of any comfort with such a man – that I should be at the hotel till one, but certainly take the mail at night.

Such was my first specimen of Mr Sheridan.

I sat musing, I remember, by my bedside for some time, miserable enough. Visions, in which I had indulged, were fast passing away, and their place was taken by others, for which I was not as yet properly prepared; – the neglect, the insults, perhaps, to which those were to be exposed, who were to go as tutors into families – the difficulties with which those were encompassed who were to have no bread to eat till they had first earned it. But it was clear what was to be done; neither respect for myself, nor prudence, admitted for a moment that I should suffer myself to be thus trifled with and thus cavalierly treated; and there was no course but to return home, however mortifying it might be, to have no other account to give my friends of my expedition, but that, far from having made an engagement with Mr Sheridan, he had not even thought it worth while to keep an appointment with me.

The next day, indeed, before the hour of one, Morris was at my hotel to assure me how concerned Sheridan was, that he had been so situated that he could neither come himself nor send a message to the St Albans; that he hoped I would put off my journey for a day and come and dine with him at Isleworth. Morris was to accompany me; – a chaise was to be ready at his house in Grosvenor-Street, to take us down, &c. &c.

I was somewhat surly and very well disposed to consult the feelings of a wounded spirit; but Morris, who was an affectionate creature, and much attached to me, was not wanting on this occasion in every soothing expression and kind expostulation. And as it at last occurred to me that I might possibly, after all, from being new to misfortune, be giving myself airs, and that I might be told so by my family, I suffered myself to be persuaded to accept the invitation, and I was in Grosvenor-Street at the hour appointed.

The house appeared to me forlorn and dirty, almost, as if uninhabited. This, it was disagreeable to observe. From the servant I found, that Mr Sheridan, ever since Mrs Sheridan's death, could not bear to live in it, and always slept at Nerot's Hotel. From Morris I had learned, that if an engagement took place, I was to live with my pupil at a house Mr Sheridan had at Wanstead. I was now going to dine with him at Isleworth; so that he appeared to have a house to dine at, another to call at, a third in which to put his family, and to have his home in none of them.

This was the second specimen I had of Mr Sheridan, and I relished it not.

I was disheartened, I confess, as I went down to Isleworth, and often regretted that I had ever left Liverpool.

But soon after we arrived Mr Sheridan drove up in his curricle, was full of apologies, all politeness and courtesy; and I was immediately struck with a sort of modesty in his manner, that I thought very remarkable and indeed very good taste, in one so celebrated.

The dinner, the afternoon, and the evening passed off, I remember, as it would have done at the house of any other gentleman, and as I lay in my bed, and not before, it occurred to me, how exquisite had been the skill of Mr Sheridan; for upon recollection I became conscious that I had chatted and talked away, just as if I had been in the company of any ordinary man, and that, while of him I perceived that I had seen little or nothing, of me in the mean time he had seen every thing, in truth, that there was to be seen. Well, I thought to myself, this is as it should be, and I turned and slept better than of late I had been accustomed to do. I saw nothing in Sheridan's countenance or appearance that indicated the man he was, except his eye, which was a sort of dark hazel, and uncommonly brilliant and expressive.

The son appeared after dinner, a fine youth, with sallow complexion and dark hair, with a quick, intelligent look and lively manner; but he was impatient to shoot swallows that were seen flitting about the river, and he soon left us.

The house had belonged to Garrick. Madam Genlis and Pamela[4] had only just left it; it was classic ground. The Thames, too, had a thousand associations belonging to it, so that Morris and I had no difficulty in amusing ourselves till Mr Sheridan might be expected to appear, which I understood was never till noon; and at noon he did appear, all smart and dressed for the day. He spoke to me with great kindness, shewed me about the place, talked to me about Madam Genlis and Pamela, and the carriages were then ordered for town. I saw him afterwards walking about the lawn in conversation with Morris. He then shook me by the hand, said he was happy to have seen me at his house, expressed a hope that I would come again, that we should be better acquainted, &c. &c.; and the carriage then drove away with me and Morris for town, while his own curricle came up to follow us.

He had allowed me to suppose from his manner that he was satisfied with me if I was with him, which he had always told Morris was indispensably necessary to both parties before any engagement could be formed. But in the mean time we were very differently situated; it was of no cosnequence to Mr Sheridan whether I chose to be tutor to his son or not; but it was very important to me, at my first outset into the world, when I had come up from Liverpool to be approved, not to return rejected.

But all thoughts of the kind were at an end from the moment that Morris had an opportunity of speaking to me in the carriage. His conversation with Mr Sheridan had been very satisfactory. I was to receive from him a business letter, as he called it; and, if my friends approved it, was to join his son at Wanstead – the sooner the better.

The letter was as handsome as possible, and I repaired to my pupil accordingly.

NOTES

After the death of his wife, Sheridan engaged William Smyth to look after his son Tom. During the whole of his engagement in that capacity, Smyth resided

with his pupil in one or other of the houses occupied by Sheridan. Smyth later became Professor of Modern History at Cambridge, and a Fellow of Peterhouse College.
1. Joseph Richardson.
2. Brooks's Club, the Whig enclave in St James's.
3. Smyth is in error about the month, since he was engaged *after* Elizabeth's death on 28 June 1793. He obviously means July.
4. Madame de Genlis and her daughter.

The Angel is Dying*

MRS STRATFORD CANNING

The circumstances attending this melancholy event were particularly distressing. A large party of young people were assembled at your brother's to spend a joyous evening in dancing.[1] We were all in the height of our merriment, – he himself remarkably cheerful, and partaking of the amusement, when the alarm was given that the dear little angel was dying. It is impossible to describe the confusion and horror of the scene: – he was quite frantic, and I knew not what to do. Happily there were present several kind, good-natured men, who had their recollection, and pointed out what should be done. We very soon had every possible assistance, and for a short time we had some hope that her precious life would have been spared to us – but that was soon at an end!

The dear babe never throve to my satisfaction: – she was small and delicate beyond imagination, and gave very little expectation of long life; but she had visibly declined during the last month.... Mr Sheridan made himself very miserable at first, from an apprehension that she had been neglected or mismanaged; but I trust he is perfectly convinced that this was not the case. He was severely afflicted at first. The dear babe's resemblance to her mother after her death was so much more striking, that it was impossible to see her without recalling every circumstance of that afflicting scene, and he was continually in the room indulging the sad remembrance. In this manner he indulged his feelings for four or five days; then, having indispensable business, he was obliged to go to London, from whence he returned, on Sunday, apparently in good spirits and as well as usual. But, however he may assume the appearance of ease or cheerfulness, his heart is not of a

* From Moore, *Memoirs of Sheridan*, II, 140. Editor's title.

nature to be quickly reconciled to the loss of any thing he loves. He suffers deeply and secretly; and I dare say he will long and bitterly lament both mother and child.

NOTES

Only one frail link remained between Sheridan and his dead wife – the child Mary, who reminded him of Eliza, and to whom he was devoted. However, the consolation which he derived from his little daughter was not long spared him. In this letter to Alicia Sheridan (Mrs Joseph Lefanu), Mrs Manning gives an account of the child's death on 23 October 1793.

1. Sheridan gave this party for his son Tom and a number of his young friends.

Pecuniary Matters*

WILLIAM SMYTH

I wrote immediately a very strong letter; and as I received no answer, I posted to town, demanded an audience, and was fully determined, after the manner of my betters, to go into the closet and resign. Certainly never did minister enter a royal apartment fuller of rage and indignation at the abominable behaviour of his sovereign master than I did the drawing-room of Mr Sheridan.

I have since often thought of the interview that passed – of the skill which Sheridan conducted himself – the patience with which he listened to my complaints, and the concern which he seemed to express, by his countenance, when I intimated to him, that though I had rather serve him for nothing than the best nobleman in the land for the best salary he could give me, still that my family were in ruins about me and that it was impossible – and that he had used me, since his intended marriage, so unceremoniously, and outraged me in a variety of ways so intolerably, that neither with proper prudence nor proper pride could I continue with him any longer; nor would I sanction, by staying with his son, any measure so contrary to my opinion, and so pregnant with ruin, as the one now resolved upon, his going to Cambridge.

To observations of this kind he for some time offered little or no

* Smyth, *Memoir of Mr Sheridan*, pp. 58–61. Editor's title.

resistance; but after I had tolerably well exhausted myself, he in his turn became the principal speaker. 'All this ruin and folly, which I entirely confess,' said he, 'originates in this one source, this marriage of mine with Miss Ogle;[1] but you know, my dear Smyth,' said he, patting me on the shoulder, 'no one is very wise on such subjects. I have no place to put her in but Wanstead. I did not consult you about Tom's going to Cambridge, for I knew you would be against it. The boy is totally ruined if you do not accompany him. It will be impossible for any one else to have any chance with him, nor should I be satisfied with any one else. I cannot put him into the army as you propose, the ministers really make such blundering expeditions. To crown all, the theatre is out of order; our last new piece, *The Iron Chest*,[2] that should have been a golden one, is really iron. And the result of my folly, my madness, if you please, is, that I am worried and tormented to death; and if you at this moment desert me and join this general combination of circumstances against me, I know not what is to become of me; and, in short, you must give me further trial, and let me see if I cannot redeem myself, and make you some amends for your kindness and consideration for me. I do not deserve it, I fully admit.'

On topics of this kind he dwelt in a manner so earnest and plausible; he so soothed and flattered me, and described what would be the situation of himself and his son if I threw up my situation, in a manner to me at the time so affecting, that my indignation began to soften, my resolution to fail me. I began to hesitate in my answers; I knew not well what to say or to think; any powers of reasoning that I ever had, seemed, on some account or other, no longer fit to serve me; and, in short, though a little sullen, I stood at least silent; and at last, like the month of March in the calendar, I came into the room like a lion and went out like a lamb. I recovered myself a little as I went down the stairs. What a clever fellow this is, I thought to myself, as I went out of the door; and, after a few paces down the street, I made one discovery more – what a fool am I.

NOTES

When tutor to Sheridan's son Tom, Smyth had ample experience of Sheridan's unreliability in pecuniary matters. Once having written to Sheridan to say that he had never got a halfpenny for teaching his son, and having obtained no answer, he determined to try what a personal interview would effect.

1. Sheridan married his second wife, Hester (Esther) Jane Ogle, on 27 April 1795.
2. *The Iron Chest* (1796), by George Colman the Younger.

A Ludicrous Line*

SAMUEL TAYLOR COLERIDGE

As an amusing anecdote, and in the wish to prepare future Authors, as young as I then was and as ignorant of the world, of the treatment they may meet with, I will add that the Person who by a twice-conveyed recommendation (in the year 1797) had urged me to write a Tragedy; who on my own objection that I was utterly ignorant of all Stage-tactics had promised that HE would himself make the necessary alterations, if the Piece should be at all representable; who together with the copy of the Play (hastened by his means so as to prevent the full development of his characters) received a letter from the Author to this purport, '*that conscious of his inexperience, he had cherished no expectations, and should therefore feel no disappointment from the rejection of the Play; but that if beyond his hopes Mr —— found in it any capacity of being adapted to the Stage, it was delivered to him as if it had been his own Manuscript, to add, omit, or alter, as he saw occasion; and that (if it were rejected) the Author would deem himself amply remunerated by the addition to his Experience which he would receive, if Mr —— would point out to him the nature of its unfitness for public Representation*'; – that this very Person returned me no answer, and, spite of repeated applications, retained my Manuscript when I was not conscious of any other Copy being in existence (my duplicate having been destroyed by an accident); that he suffered this Manuscript to wander about the Town from his house . . . likewise that the same person asserted (as I have been assured) that the Play was rejected because I would not submit to the alteration of one ludicrous line; and finally in the 1806 amused and delighted (as who was ever in his company, if I may trust the universal report, without being amused and delighted?) a large company at the house of a highly respectable Member of Parliament, with the ridicule of the Tragedy, as 'a *fair specimen*' of the *whole* of which he adduced a line: 'Drip! drip! drip! there's nothing here but dripping.'

In the original copy of the Play, in the first Scene of the fourth Act, Isidore *had* commenced his Soliloquy in the Cavern with the words, 'Drip! drip! a ceaseless sound of water-drops', as far as I can at present recollect:[1] for on the possible ludicrous association being pointed out to me, I instantly and thankfully struck out the line. And as to my

---

* Samuel Taylor Coleridge, *Remorse* (London: W. Pople, 1813) pp. 3fn. Editor's title.

obstinate *tenancity*, not only my old acquaintance, but (I dare boldly aver) both the Managers of Drury-Lane Theatre, and every Actor and Actress, whom I have recently met in the Green-room, will repel the accusation; perhaps not without surprise.

NOTES

Sheridan had once been an aspiring author, dependent on the good will of a theatre manager; now, he was a manager himself and the fate of other authors was in his hands. Their manuscripts, which he never showed much inclination to read, heaped up on his table, and the day came when Samuel Taylor Coleridge (1772–1834), exasperated beyond endurance by Sheridan's endless procrastination and evasiveness over his own manuscript of *Osorio*, set him down as 'an unprincipled rogue'.

1. It appears that Coleridge's memory or his ingenuousness is somewhat at fault here, for the fourth act of the play in its original shape opened with the following lines:

> Drip! drip! drip! drip! – in such a place as this
> It has nothing else to do but drip! drip! drip!
> I wish it had not dripp'd upon my torch.

Sheridan Called*

LADY BESSBOROUGH

Cav[endish] Sq[ua]re,
Tuesday [August]

... I pass'd a very different day from what I had plann'd. Sheridan call'd in the morning and found out that I was alone, and told me he would dine with me. I thought, of course, he was in joke, but, point du tout,[1] he arriv'd at dinner, din'd, and staid the whole evening. He was very pleasant, but – it was not you, and the seeing anybody only increas'd my regrets, which I suppose were pretty visible, for every five minutes he kept saying how I am wasting all my efforts to entertain

---

* From Lord Granville Leveson Gower (First Earl Granville), *Private Correspondence, 1781 to 1821*, ed. Castalia Countess Granville (London: John Murray, 1916) I, 216. Editor's title.

you, while you are grieving that you cannot change me into *Ld Levison*. You would not be so grim if he was beaming on you. At length, as I thought he was preparing to pass the night as well as the eve^g with me, and as he began some fine speeches I did not quite approve of, I order'd my Chair, to get rid of him. This did not succeed, for as I had no place to go to, he follow'd me about to Anne's and Ly D——s [Duncannon's] where I knew I should not be let in, and home again. But, luckily, I got in time enough to order every one to be denied, and ran up stairs, while I heard him expostulating with the porter. . . .

NOTES

Sheridan's relations with Lady Bessborough became so notorious that her injured husband began a suit in Doctor's Commons against the erring pair, and it was only with great difficulty that he was persuaded to relinquish it. Lady Bessborough was the Duchess of Devonshire's sister, and is well remembered as the mother of Lady Caroline Lamb; she lived to be referred to by the resentful and irreverent Byron as old Lady Blarney. This letter was written to Lord Granville Leveson Gower in 1798.
   1. Not at all.

Sheridan Called Again*
LADY BESSBOROUGH

23 August.
Here I am quite alone in C[avendish] Square. We came Saturday as I told you, and staid on to see my Sister[1] set out. I was oblig'd to stay for a Christening, and as Ld B[essborough] was engag'd to dine and sleep at Mortlake, I remain to do some commissions for my Sister. I din'd at Ly Melbourne's, but would not go with her to the play and Vauxhall as she wanted; but came quietly home regretting that I had nothing to expect . . . no carriage to watch for, no rap at the door . . . and alas! no chance of hearing your Step upon the stair. . . . Whilst I was regretting all this, suddenly the knock did come, to my utter astonishment. I ran to the stair, and in a moment heard Sheridan's Voice. I do not know why, but I took a horror of seeing him, and

---

* From Leveson Gower, *Private Correspondence, 1781 to 1821*, I, 350–1. Editor's title.

hurried Sally down to say I was out. I heard him answer: 'Tell her I call'd twice this morning and want particularly to see her, for I know she is at home.' Sally protested I was out, and S. answer'd: 'Then I shall walk up and down before the door till she comes in', and there he is walking sure enough. It is partly all the nonsense he talk'd all this year and the hating to see any one, when I cannot see you, that makes me dislike letting him in so much. There was a time when I was not afraid of him; he amus'd me, and I could laugh at his manner, as I do at Hare's[2] or any one's, but now I feel the justice of some of his attacks. . . .

I left off writing that I might not make a lamentation de Jérémie,[3] and weary you with it. S. call'd again after walking up and down for near an hour, and I sent down word I was sorry I could not see him, but that I was not well. I am not in a humour to be flatter'd or abus'd, frighten'd or complimented, and he is in one – I know by what he said to my Sister and Hare – to torment me instead of amusing me, which he can do if he pleases. I wonder how long Sheridan, Ld John, and Fitzpatrick will think it necessary to make love to me whenever we chance to meet, cela ne sied ni à leur âge ni au mien,[4] and if they mean it for flattery, it has quite the contrary effect, and troubles me more than the worst abuse could. Were I much younger I should be asham'd and provok'd, but *now*, if it were not that they expose themselves more than me, I should think it was to laugh at me.

NOTES

This letter was written to Lord Granville Leverson Gower in 1802.
1. Georgiana, Duchess of Devonshire.
2. James Hare.
3. Lamentation of Jeremiah.
4. This befits neither their age nor mine.

Recollections of Sheridan*

JOHN PHILIP KEMBLE

The winter season of 1784–5 opened with one favourable circumstance, the return of Mr King[1] to Drury Lane Theatre. He accepted the management of the stage, disclaiming, however, very particularly, the having any power whatever as to the acceptance or rejection of the usual literary offerings to the theatre. This department was principally assumed by Mr Sheridan himself, who had neither leisure nor inclination to attend to it. Melancholy proofs of this appeared in piles of long forgotten tragedies and comedies, which he had promised to consider, and had never opened. Mr Kemble, whom I one day found sitting very patiently in this great man's library, pointed to this *funeral* pile, and added to his action the declaration of his belief, that in these morning attendances, he had read more of these productions than ever had been or would be read by the proprietor himself.

Sheridan's habit was to keep his visitors distributed variously, according to their rank or intimacy with him. Some, like ourselves, penetrated into the library; others tired the chairs in the parlour; and the tradesmen lost their time in the hall, the butler's room, and other scenical divisions of the premises. A door opening above stairs, moved all the hopes below: but when he came down his hair was drest for the day, and his countenance for the occasion; and so cordial were his manners, his glance so masterly, and his address so captivating, that the people, for the most part, seemed to forget what they actually wanted, and went away, as if they had come only to look at him. This is, in truth, here written by anticipation; at this time, I had not the honour to be known to Mr Sheridan. . . .

Now, at this time, Sheridan was playing the game of ambition for the very largest stake. In the impeachment of Warren Hastings, he came forward to blaze with a brightness that should eclipse all ancient, as well as modern, eloquence. His father had published a rhetorical grammar:[2] the son, in Westminster Hall, was to exemplify the whole art of rhetoric, not so much in the hope of convicting that injured man,

---

* From James Boaden, *Memoirs of the Life of John Philip Kemble* (London: Longman *et al.*, 1825), I, 203–4, 409–12; II, 74–7, 344–5. Editor's title.

Mr Hastings (for the managers always knew him to be safe), but as, in fact, the real puppets of the superior policy of Mr Pitt; who having by *his* India bill robbed them of the patronage of India, delivered over the India Company to their persecution, so that he might still hold the East under his protection; while he diverted, by so severe a labour, the talents of opposition from too constant an attention to his own measures as minister. The nabobs, therefore, detested the Opposition for seeking to dry up the streams, that flowed with fortunes to them. The nation saw nothing but personal spleen in the managers, which in its indulgence was to cost them an immense sum of money; and the sole result, a grand theatrical display in the new theatre of Westminster Hall; where months of dry evidence were now and then diversified by a day's eloquence on either side, for the amusement of those, who from right or courtesy had the tickets of admission.

Nor was the impeachment the only subject to draw away the attention of Mr Sheridan from the theatre. The King's alarming indisposition was itself a circumstance to rivet him to the objects of his party. Their Majesties, on Tuesday the 28th of October, had honoured the Countess of Effingham with a morning visit. In the evening the King found himself unwell with a nervous complaint, from which Sir G. Baker thought he might soon recover, but he recommended that His Majesty should not come to town. The nation became soon seriously alarmed; and the question arose, upon the ascertainment of the King's condition, called the question of the regency; upon which, in the enforcement of the speculative *right* of the heir-apparent, doctrine repugnant to common sense was affirmed to be the spirit of the British constitution. Mr Pitt again, upon this question, conducted himself with a prudence, which routed all the forcing claims set up by the Opposition; but the contest was long and arduous, and while the heavier ordnance of the party kept up a constant discharge upon the cabinet, Mr Sheridan seemed to have assumed to himself the lighter warfare of personal annoyance, and laboured with but indifferent success, though with great address, to irritate the temper of Mr Pitt. By doing this it was imagined the haughty spirit of the minister might lead him to say something offensive to the illustrious substitute for the Sovereign, and render it impossible for him ever to listen to the claims of Mr Pitt and his colleagues. The leaders of Opposition were considered to be the personal friends of the Prince of Wales; but they were anxious to take security against the change, which power is apt to create in such attachments.

Thus on every side was Mr Sheridan forcibly drawn from dramatic objects. For the nightly combats of the House of Commons, the quickness of his mind supplied abundant stores; but the displays upon the India question could not be made without the most elaborate preparation; and though he left the general interest to the zeal and comprehensive grasp of Mr Burke, yet with Mr Sheridan's habits it was matter of wonder, how he could render himself master of the knowledge displayed by him on the Begum charge. He was, for the most part, as accurate as eloquent; but if at this distance of time, I were to fix upon a matter of peculiar praise to him, I should celebrate his *urbanity*. In speaking of actions, he characterised them as they seemed to him; but he never spoke as an enemy: he was a prosecutor, never a persecutor; and good taste in him gave the tone to public duty. . . .

Mr Kemble, as it has been stated, found himself greatly annoyed in his management; and he attributed his impediments to the indolence, often – oftener, I think, to the yielding good humour, of Sheridan. He was, with the greatest difficulty, induced to retain his situation. Matters were carried, in defiance of his judgement, and thus there were persons encouraged to contemn his authority. I was present one night in Suffolk Street, when he denounced his fixed, his unalterable determination. He expected Sheridan there after the house should be up, and aware of the great disarming powers of the orator, in a sort of inarticulate murmur, alarmed the party with the prospect of a scene; and as some very excellent claret was near him, he proceeded to fortify himself for the engagement. At length Sheridan arrived, took his place next to Mrs Crouch[3] at the table, looked at Kemble with kindness, but the kindness was neither returned nor acknowledged. The great actor now looked unutterable things, and occasionally emitted a *humming* sound like that of a bee, and groaned in the spirit inwardly. Crouch whispered two words in Sheridan's ear, which let him know, I believe, the *exact* cause of the present moody appearance of his manager. A considerable time elapsed, and frequent repetitions of the sound before mentioned occurred; when at last, 'like a pillar of state', slowly up rose Kemble, and in these words addressed the astonished proprietor. 'I am an EAGLE, whose wings have been bound down by frosts and snows; but now I shake my pinions, and cleave into the general air, unto which I am born.' He then deliberately resumed his seat, and looked as if he had relieved himself from insupportable thraldom. Sheridan knew the complacency of man under the notion of a fine figure, and saw that his eagle was not absolutely irreclaimable; he rose, took a chair next to the great actor; in two minutes resumed his old ascendency. The tragedian soon softened into his usual forgiving temper; and I am ashamed to say how late it was when, cordial as brothers, I took one arm of Kemble, and Sheridan the other, and resolutions were formed 'that melted as breath into the passing wind'.

And such WAS the power of Sheridan upon this and every occasion. With Kemble he might be said to have a friend in the citadel, for that good man's veneration for him was extreme; and most certainly I never heard him speak with equal warmth of any other existing talent. Of politics he knew absolutely nothing; of passing events scarcely anything. Newspapers he did not read: so that when I occasionally repeated to him, what I had heard from Mr Pitt, or read in the publications of Burke, he always recurred to his grand theme, the eloquence of Sheridan; and, as Mrs Kemble often said, on that subject he was an inveterate idolater. Yet he sometimes threw off his allegiance. 'I know him thoroughly,' he said; 'all his sophistry, all his paltry artifices – but I will become a member of his own society, the FRIENDS of the PEOPLE; and when he rises to speak, I'll PUT HIM DOWN.' These were only the ebullitions of disappointed attachment and rooted affection; and having persuaded himself of a very extraordinary likeness that Sheridan bore to the countenance of Shakespeare, I incline to think, if Mr Kemble had formed a scale of which the author of Hamlet was at the summit, the next degree, among the fervours of genius, would have been occupied by the author of *The School for Scandal*. . . .

On the 9th of June, Mr Richardson,[4] one of the proprietors of Drury Lane, died from the effects of a ruptured blood-vessel. I formerly touched with regret upon the early close of a life, that might, under a change of habits, have been highly useful, as it was certainly ornamental. I noticed that he had his full share in the classical pleasantries of his time. He was a contributor, with Ellis and Dr Lawrence, to the *Rolliad* and *Probationary Odes*. My pleasant and constant friend through life, Mr Taylor, knew Richardson well before the spell of Sheridan took hold upon him; and has fondly described him to me as one of the gayest spirits about town. A man of lively imagination, great reading, sound judgement, and possessing an almost unerring perception of character.

Richardson once said a strong thing of Sheridan: 'It was his sincere conviction, that could some enchanter's wand touch him into the possession of fortune, he would instantly convert him into a being of the nicest honour, and most unimpeachable moral excellence.' Riches are so often quoted as the corrupters of our nature, that I could not suppress even a *fancy* of their moral efficacy.

Sheridan had for Richardson all the affection that a careless man can have for any thing. He made a point, therefore, of going down to Egham, to see the last offices performed over his remains. Mr Taylor says, they arrived too late by about a quarter of an hour. The clergyman had just retired from the grave. Sheridan was in an agony of grief at this disappointment; but his powerful *name*, properly enforced upon the rector, procured a polite and humane repetition of the close of the service, to enable the tardy orator to say that he had attended the funeral of his friend.

The party dined together at the Inn, and after the cloth was removed, their kindness for the deceased broke forth in *designed* testimonials to his merits. Dr Combe was to choose the kind of stone for his mausoleum, and Sheridan himself undertook to compose a suitable inscription; but no curious stone ever covered his remains, and the promised inscription never was written. Such are the hasty pledges of recent grief, and the performances of indolent genius.

NOTES

John Philip Kemble (1757–1823), English actor; brother of actress Sarah Siddons.

    1. Thomas King.
    2. Thomas Sheridan, *A Course of Lectures on Elocution* (London, 1762; privately printed).
    3. The actress.
    4. Joseph Richardson died on 9 June 1803. Sheridan fell into an agony of tears at his loss.

Recollections of Sheridan*

ELIZABETH LADY HOLLAND

Sheridan was expected to have made a capital speech in the H. of Commons on the Union last week, but it was reckoned very inferior to his usual style of excellence. He offended the seceders by announcing that the standard of Opposition would soon be unfurled.[1] He introduced it at the conclusion of an attack upon Ld L[ansdown], who had, he said, 'cut a clumsy caper over the grave of party'. (In his speech at the beginning of the session, he said, 'Thank God, party is dead and buried.') He pursued a strain of irony, apparently levelled at Ld L., but, in fact, intended for [George] Tierney, who had, in a late speech,

---

* *The Journal of Elizabeth Lady Holland*, ed. the Earl of Ilchester (London: Longman, Green, 1908) I, 220–4, 255, 278–9; II, 80–1. Editor's title.

declared that he considered himself as an individual belonging to no set of men. Sheridan said, he did not wonder party was denied, for it required strong intellect to command, and great virtues to attach for a man to become the leader of party, and great humility and sense to fall as a subaltern into the ranks of party. Sheridan hates Tierney. That hatred was roused at T's making a most excellent speech on ye Income Bill. It was so good that everybody praised it. S. was at Brooks's, and was so incensed at the applause that he went to Tierney's house, whom he found just getting into bed, insisted upon seeing him, and then said he was quite shocked to hear that a part of his speech had given great offence, that part where he hinted at the necessity of squeezing the corporations, who were 'wallowing in wealth'. This was said to worry Tierney, who is weakly alive to all unpopularity. T. told me this himself.

Ld Lansdown is just returned from Bath. He was full of what Miss Fox calls *effusion* to Ld H[olland], who had said that he regretted the probability of their voting against each other upon the subject of the Union. 'Never mind,' said Ld L., 'vote, speak against me, abuse me. Do what you will. I should say, this is what I can't hear, I can't see; I won't see it. You are like my sons who can't offend me, for I won't quarrel with them.' In short, he was all tenderness and warmth.

Sheridan offended the Prince extremely in his last speech. I do not know precisely what he said, but it was a quotation from Secretary Cooke's pamphlet. He certainly intended it as complimentary, but it was not probably faithfully reported by P. Ernest to ye Prince, and before S. could tell his own story, the Prince, with his usual intemperance and violence, abused him, calling him 'rogue, liar', etc. This *malentendu*[2] will vex S. beyond measure, for he has ever since the Regency courted the P., and anticipated in imagination much influence in a future reign; besides that he has wished to be considered as being as much the organ of the P. in the H. of Commons as Ld Moira is in the House of Lords. I have malignity enough in my disposition not to feel much sympathy for his afflictions. He has afflicted so much real distress upon others, and one being dear to me, that I have not a spark of compassion to bestow. His defenders (and their number is but slender) say that all his bad conduct has proceeded from his struggling against the meanness of his origin and the littleness of his means. He attempted to efface the first by distinguishing himself, not only in the career of wit and politics, but also in that of gallantry and fashion; for such was his lust of praise that: –

> Women and fools must like him or he dies;
> The wond'ring Senates hung on all he spoke,
> The Club must hail him Master of the Joke.

> Enough if all around him but admire.

I shall note down a few ancedotes about him by-and-bye.

Ld H. met at Sheridan's, one day lately, Mr Pollen, the man who dreaded invasion for the sake of the chastity of the ladies: he had never seen him before. Ld H. was telling a story to prove the openness of the Irish character, and how little suspicious they were of trusting their lives to a person of tolerable character. The story was told him by Ld Wycombe as having happened to an acquaintance of his – a Mr Henry. A man arrested him in the streets, and, without much prefatory discourse asked him if he would be of the *Executive*, adding, he was a United Irishman, and was delegated by those sitting in Dublin to ask him. Upon which Mr Pollen immediately said: 'The same thing precisely occurred to me at Perth. A United Scotsman proposed the same question, altho' I was in my regimentals, and he knew I was quartered with my regiment.' The coincidence was remarkable, but tho' Scotsmen are more wary than Irishmen, yet it was possible there might be an indiscreet Scot. They then talked of poor Ld Lauderdale, who is dreadfully ill. His complaint is a horrid one, a local dropsy, which he will not submit to have properly treated, upon which Mr P. said, 'There are two modes of treating the disease: there is the palliative and the radical. I first tried the palliative, but it was troublesome, and ever since I used the radical I have felt no inconvenience.' Ld H. said he began to stare at two such extraordinary things having been mentioned, and that both should have happened to him. He is not above 25 or 26, and that disorder is generally in old, wornout constitutions, and, if one may judge from Gibbon's averseness to mention the complaint, is not one that men are apt to boast of having. . . . Ld H. was all astonishment at these stories, but upon inquiry he found Mr Pollen's nickname was 'Prodigy' Pollen.

Wednesday, 13th. Feb. – On Sunday, ye 10th, Mr [James] Hare came to pass a few days. On Wednesday Bor. and Amherst died. On last Sunday Hare returned. [Lord Charles] Grey and Tierney dined. Miss Fox stayed from Saturday to Monday.

Hare was full of wit and pleasantry. I was expressing surprise that a man so universally extolled for his conversation and talents should not, to my taste, be pleasant, for the fact is, I never received the smallest entertainment from Sheridan's convivial abilities. Hare said what is true enough, that before women he is always playing a game. His forte is at a club over wine, and in debate. Among many things he told us of a reply of S., in debate, to Dundas,[3] who had asserted a falsehood for a fact, and supported it by some well-known trite joke. S. complimented the honble gentleman upon his abilities, especially upon possessing to a remarkable degree a *retentive memory* and *fertile imagination*, but that those faculties unfortunately were perverted, as his memory was directed to works of imagination, and his imagination to facts. S. himself, however, is less tenacious about facts than he ought to be. There is a story of his offering some stories to Mr Fox, to assist him in argument, but the latter, who is very strict as to what he asserts, asked if they were well authenticated, and, finding they depended upon report, declined using them; upon which S. said, 'He is so d——d *surly about facts.*'

S. was to have dined here on Sunday, but did not; probably to avoid meeting Tierney and Grey, as he hates the former, and is displeased at not being supported by the latter. His motion very nearly failed, as nobody seconded it for full 10 minutes, and then an obscure man jumped up and did it. All their squabbles are diverting, for as to any good they can do, it is a farce to suppose any can be done. This Union, they say, is to be carried at all risks. Ld H. is gone this morning to arrange with Ld Fitzwilliam, but the subject is so tiresome, and I have heard so much of it, that I cannot enter into the merits or demerits of the case. . . .

Went on Monday to *Pizarro*,[4] Sheridan and Tierney, Addeley, etc. The first came into my box perpetually to explain whenever there was a failure in the representation. I was surprised at his eagerness, and glad to find that drinking has not so totally absorbed his faculties, and that he is still sensible to fame. About him my reason and impulse always are at variance; reflection convinces me he ought to be despised for his private life and doubted for his political, but whenever I see him, if but for five minutes, a sort of cheerful frankness and pleasant wittiness puts to flight all ye reasonable prejudices that I entertain against him. . . .

I had a long walk upon the terrace with Tierney. I was in an eloquent *veine*, and happily conveyed all I intended to express without the rigorous exterior of forbidding prudery. I think I convinced him his attentions offended and his hopes insulted me, that I was firmly attached at home, and tho' I felt at present no resentment towards him, yet I should if his pretensions continued. On Thursday Ld H. dined at the Tower; Ld T. [Lord Townshend] is confined by a fit of the gout. Sheridan was of their party; he is just come from 'Peruvianising', that is from the country. He is so delighted with *Pizarro* that his allusions are taken from it in everything he says. He said ye 10th of July was so delicious, something in the temperature so bewitching and tempting to go astray and follow ye dictates of nature, that if he were to sit in judgement upon a cause of gallantry, if the indictment stated it as committed on ye 10th of July, he would go into the evidence, but instantly bring in *Guilty, by the visitation of God*. . . .

The papers on Friday announced a singular accident which happened to the King at the Review on Thursday in Hyde Park; a musket ball wounded a Mr Ongley standing near him. The question was whether it was from design or chance – the chance of an unloaded musket. When I came home, the first question I asked the porter in getting out of my carriage was whether there was anything new; he replied with eager alarm that the King had been shot at from a pistol at the play. I thought this story an exaggeration of the former one, but to my surprise found that the evening of the day on which he had escaped the bullet, he was deliberately aimed at from the pit. The ball lodged in the upper boxes, and the King escaped unhurt. His behaviour was like that of a hero of antiquity; he was in full possession of all his faculties, and was cool enough to tell the Queen, who was not in the box when the pistol was fired, that the report was from a squib. He remained on during the play with the utmost sang-froid. He told a person that he observed the fiddlers expected another shot as they covered their heads with their cremonas. The enthusiasm was boundless; additional verses were added by Sheridan to *God Save the King*.[5] The King was so delighted with Sheridan's behaviour to the Princesses, for he prevented them going into their box by saying that a pickpocket was taken in the pit which made a riot and his presence was required, and begged their R[oyal] H[ighnesses] to wait in the room. He shall feel gratitude to the latest hour of his life, he says, to him for this sensibility. Sheridan, Mrs S., and Tom are all to go to Court, both to-morrow and Thursday.

NOTES

Elizabeth Lady Holland (1770?–1845), English society hostess.
   1. On 22 January 1799. 'The banner of party is furled, but it is not beaten down. I trust that it will again be displayed and that it will assemble round it the steady friends to true liberty, hostile alike to despotic rule, and to wild innovation.'
   2. Misunderstanding.
   3. Henry Dundas, 1st Viscount Melville.
   4. *Pizarro* was produced on 24 May 1799.

5. From every latent foe,
   From the assassin's blow,
     God save the King!
   O'er him thine arm extend,
   For Britain's sake defend
   Our father, prince, and friend,
     God save the King!

Never Sober*

LADY BESSBOROUGH

Poor Richardson is dead. Sheridan (if Richardson's death does not frighten him) will do the same, for he is never sober for a moment; and his affairs, worse than ever. *Pour comble*,[1] he has quarrelled with Mrs S. A sort of separation took place, but I believe it is partly made up again – at least I believe they live in the same house again, but not very good friends.[2] I am very sorry for it, for she was the only chance there was of stopping his drinking.

NOTES

By 1803, Sheridan's second wife Esther, like his first wife Elizabeth, was demanding separation; and although she too was shortly reconciled to him, he was in so distressed a condition that Lady Bessborough was alarmed, as can be seen in this letter to Lord Holland.

1. Worst of all.
2. 'By my life and soul,' Sheridan wrote to his wife on 30 June 1803, 'if you will talk of leaving me now you will destroy me. I am wholly unwell and neither sleep nor eat.'

---

* From Sichel, *Sheridan, from New and Original Material*, II, 270. Editor's title.

Dick's Astonishment*

CHARLES FRANCIS SHERIDAN

Dick, according to custom, was the last person who came; but before he entered the room the Prince communicated the scheme to the other gentlemen. When Dick came into the room I took care to keep my back towards him and Tom;[1] as to Charles,[2] neither Dick nor Tom knew him, and as there was very little light in the room, Master Dick, after paying his respects to the Prince, and speaking to the other gentlemen with whom he was acquainted, began to stare at Charles and me as at two persons perfectly strangers to him, and with a look of wonder, as if astonished at finding at one of the Prince's most private and friendly dinner-parties, two men he had never seen in his life before; the Prince then burst out into a violent [laugh?], as did the other gentlemen, without speaking a word. This wonderfully increased Dick's astonishment, and he made so ludicrous an appearance that it was with the utmost difficulty I avoided laughing also, which would have immediately betrayed me to Dick. The Prince then called out to the other gentlemen, 'I have taken Sheridan in. I have been these ten years desiring him to bring his brother to see me without succeeding, and now I have the pleasure of being acquainted with his brother, without his assistance.' Upon this I turned round short upon Master Richard – never did human being look so surprised and at the same time so confused – the laugh, at the same time, was renewed with increased violence, and in the midst of the noise the awkwardness of our meeting was witnessed by nobody. Dick then took me aside to make me a thousand shuffling apologies, not worth mentioning, for not having been to see me, and dinner being announced saved me the trouble of telling him I did not believe one word he said. I did not sit near him at dinner; and being in tolerable spirits, and he, I believe, really ashamed of himself, I took the lead of him in the conversation at starting and kept it the whole time that we remained at table, except when the Prince spoke. He talked much and well, and is, I think, one of the pleasantest companions I ever met with. I had the good luck to set him in a roar of laughter, as well as the rest of the company several times, and as I was new, Master Richard was kept in the background by the tacit consent of the company. In the course of the evening I

---

* *Temple Bar* (London), 119 (March 1900) 408–9. Editor's title.

became as well acquainted with the Prince as if I had known him these twenty years, and he treated me as if he had known me as long. In short I had the good luck to please him and the rest of [the] gentlemen, who were strangers to me, and who all desired to have the honour of cultivating my acquaintance, and took down my address. The Prince was so particularly obliging and attentive to me, and frequently applauded so much what I said, he so often repeated how happy he was at having at length obtained the pleasure of making my acquaintance, and his desire and wishes that he should see me very often, that it was impossible I could have had a more compleat triumph over Master Richard for his unfeeling neglect than this day produced to me – so much so, that tho' Charles was very angry with him before, he told me, when the company broke up, that he almost pitied poor Dick.

NOTES

In March 1804, Sheridan's brother Charles Francis (1750–1806) was in London and had an opportunity at last to meet the Prince of Wales at a dinner party. He gives an account of this meeting in a letter to his wife. Charles Sheridan made his career in Irish politics. He was ambitious and able like his younger brother, but without Dick's charm or brilliance.
1. Richard Brinsley's son.
2. Charles Sheridan, Charles Francis's son.

I Thought I Knew Brinsley*

CHARLES FRANCIS SHERIDAN

I agree in opinion with you, my dearest Love, and am more decided in the opinion than you appear to be that I may lay the foundation of much future good by this trip to London – for long as I have known and well as I thought I knew Brinsley – I find I had still to learn the full extent of his want of those feelings that can constitute him even a friend much less a brother. I never was before convinced that no sort of reliance whatever can be placed upon him, and that all I had sacrificed in the political line would, with his hearty goodwill, have

* *Temple Bar* (London), 119 (March 1900) 409–10. Editor's title.

remained for ever unrewarded and unnoticed, if it in the slightest degree depended upon *him*, that it should be acknowledged. I therefore most prodigiously miscalculated, when I imagined, as I confess I once did imagine, that my having a brother on the spot, would in some degree do away the mischief of my absence from London, and that his constant presence, and as constant intercourse with those who in future will be all powerful, would be a sort of substitute for my own presence, remedy or obviate the injury to my interests, which my constant absence would otherwise induce. It is a point of no small importance that I have discovered my error in time, it is one of still greater, that I have had an opportunity of establishing my claims on my *own account* totally independent of him, and that those claims have been allowed in the quarter, where I most wished to have them allowed, and I have every reason to be assured will be considered, whether Mr Brinsley were to continue in existence or not.

NOTE

Another letter from Charles Francis Sheridan to his wife, containing information about himself, and further comments of a disparaging kind upon his younger brother, Richard Brinsley.

A Difficult Position*

THOMAS CREEVEY

Among other persons who came to pay their respects to the Prince during the Autumn of 1805 was Mr Hastings, whom I had never seen before excepting at his trial in Westminster Hall. He and Mrs Hastings came to the Pavilion, and I was present when the Prince introduced Sheridan to him, which was curious, considering that Sheridan's parliamentary fame had been built upon his celebrated speech against Hastings. However, he lost no time in attempting to cajole old Hastings, begging him to believe that any part he had ever taken against him was purely political, and that no one had a greater respect for him than himself, &c, &c, upon which old Hastings said with great gravity that 'it would be a great consolation to him in his declining days if Mr

* *The Creevey Papers* (London: John Murray, 1903) I, 59–60. Editor's title.

Sheridan would make that sentence more publick'; but Sheridan was obliged to mutter and get out of such engagements as well as he could.

NOTE

The trial of Warren Hastings dragged over eight years, and on 23 April 1795 he was acquitted on all charges brought against him. Ten years later Sheridan met him at Brighton, when he was a guest of the Prince of Wales. The position was one of difficulty, and Thomas Creevey, MP (1768–1838), recorded the incident with a malicious smile.

A Distressing Evening*

ANNE MATHEWS

About this period [1808] Mr Mathews first saw the Prince of Wales at a fête given to his Royal Highness by Mr Abraham Goldsmidt, at Merton. My husband at first hesitated to accept the invitation, and for some time balanced between his desire to meet the great personage he much wished to see, and the fear that he might be asked for the purpose, when there, of contributing to his entertainment. He consulted Mr [John] Braham, who removed his fears. . . . The invitation was therefore accepted, and no indication was given of any such design as my husband had at first suspected. At supper he managed to sit next to Mr Braham at a table remote from that at which the Prince sat, and where several of his familiar friends were also assembled. All apprehensions of any annoyance having long before subsided, he was cheerfully enjoying hismelf with his friends, when he felt a tap upon his shoulder, and received the next moment an intimation in the following form from his host: 'Mr Mathews, you must go with me to the other table; the Prince wants you.' To this curious mode of address my husband replied, 'Impossible, Mr Goldsmidt; I cannot think of going.' 'But,' added his host, 'he has asked for you; you must go', meaning to say, 'etiquette requires you to obey the command of royalty'. Poor Mr Mathews sickened at the thought, and appealed to Braham, who gravely filled up the measure of his discontent by coolly

---

* Mrs Anne Mathews, *Life and Correspondence of Charles Mathews, the Elder, Comedian* (London, 1860) pp. 124–5. Editor's title.

replying, 'You must go.' Accordingly, away he went with his host, who left him near the table where the royal guest was seated. He was hesitating what to do (for there was no vacant seat), when Mr Goldsmidt rejoined him, and with less delicacy than eagerness to gratify his Royal Highness, called out aloud, 'Mr Mathews, Mr Mathews, stand opposite the Prince – stand opposite; the Prince wants to look at you!' His Royal Highness seemed quite shocked at this rather coarse version of his desire, and did not at the moment forget that he was England's gentleman, for, with a hurried and even embarrassed manner, he said, as he bent forward across the table, 'I am very happy to be introduced to you, Mr Mathews, but there's no seat that side.' The Prince then turned to Mr Sheridan, who was next him, and said, 'Sheridan, can't we make a seat for Mathews between us?' at the same time contracting his own and making a space, he pressed my husband between himself and Mr Sheridan.

NOTE

This recollection by Mrs Mathews of her husband Charles Mathews, the comedian, shows that Sheridan at that time was at the right hand of the Prince of Wales.

Recollections of Sheridan*

MICHAEL KELLY

Mr Sheridan gave a dinner at the Piazza Coffee House to Mr [Henry] Holland, the architect of New Drury, and a number of his friends were present on the occasion; amongst others invited, Mr [John Philip] Kemble, [Stephen] Storace, and myself. I happened to be placed near Mr Sheridan, who at that time knew very little of me except my being one of his performers; in the course of the evening, he was lamenting to me, the situation the theatre was placed in by the illness and absence of some of its leading performers, and wished me to suggest what operatic piece could be got up without them. After a little thought, I proposed to him to get up *Cymon*, which could be done without any of

* *Reminiscences of Michael Kelly* (London: Henry Colburn, 1826) II, 17–256. Editor's title.

the absent performers. Mr Sheridan replied, '*Cymon*, my good Sir, would not bring sixpence to the treasury.'

'Granted, Sir,' said I, '*Cymon* as it now stands certainly might not; but my reason for proposing it, is, that I saw at Naples an opera, at the end of which, was a grand procession and tournament, triumphal cars, drawn by horses, giants, dwarfs, leopards, lions, and tigers, which was eminently successful; and it is my opinion that *Cymon* might be made a vehicle for the introduction of a similar spectacle. I recollect all the spectacle part as done at Naples; and I think, with the novelty of your present theatre, and the manner in which the piece can be cast, *Cymon* would bring a mint of money to the house.'

After a moment's reflection, he said he thought it would, that he felt obliged to me for the suggestion, and that he would give directions to have it brought forward with all possible speed. The evening was spent with great good humour; my friend, Jack Bannister, contributed to its hilarity, by giving us excellent imitations of several of the performers of both theatres. At the conclusion, we adjourned to another room to take coffee; as Kemble was walking somewhat majestically towards the door, and Jack Bannister getting up to go after him, I hallooed out, 'Bannister, follow that lord, but see you mock him not', as Bannister, a moment before, had been mocking the actors; the quotation was thought rather apt, and produced much laughter.

Mr Sheridan told Storace that night, that he was very much pleased with me, and desired him to bring me the Sunday following to dine with him in Bruton Street; he did so, and surprising to relate, Mr Sheridan was at home to receive us. I spent a delightful day; and, after that, to the lamented day of that great man's death, I had the happiness to enjoy his confidence and society. Great preparations were made to prepare *Cymon*; no expense was spared; and the piece was produced with all splendour and magnificence. . . .

In the summer of 1793, Mrs Crouch and I had engagements at Birmingham, Manchester, Chester, Shrewsbury, Worcester, and Liverpool; and at Dublin, for December, January, and February.

Previous to going there, we played a few nights at Liverpool. My benefit was the last night of our engagement. In the morning of that eventful day, crossing Williamson Square to go to the theatre, a gentleman stopped me, and accosting me with the most pointed civility, informed me that he had a writ against me for 350*l.*; I, at the time, not owing a sixpence to any living creature.

I said he must be mistaken in his man. He shewed me the writ which was at the suit of a Mr Henderson, an upholsterer in Coventry-street; and the debt, he said, had been incurred for furnishing the

Opera House with covering for the boxes, pit, &c, &c. So, instead of preparing for the custody of Locket, on the stage, (for *The Beggar's Opera* was the piece to be acted), I was obliged to go to a spunging-house.

I requested the sheriff's officer, who was extremely civil, to accompany me to Mrs Crouch, to consult what I had best do; she advised me by no means to acknowledge the debt, but to go to the Exchange, and state publicly the cause of my arrest, and to ask any gentleman there to become bail; making over to such bail, as a security, nearly five hundred pounds, which we luckily had paid into Mr Heywood's bank, in Liverpool, three days before; but Mr Frank Aickin, who was then manager, rendered any such arrangement unnecessary, as he very handsomely came forward and bailed me. I was therefore released, and performed Macheath that night to a crowded house.

I sent my servant to London by the mail, with an account of the transaction to Mr Sheridan, who immediately settled the debt in his own peculiar way. He sent for Henderson the upholsterer, to his house; and after describing the heinous cruelty he had committed, by arresting a man who had nothing to do with the debt, and who was on a professional engagement in the country, expatiated and remonstrated, explained and extenuated, until he worked so much upon the upholsterer, that in less than half an hour, he agreed to exonerate me and my bail; taking, instead of such security, Mr Sheridan's bond; which, I must say, was extremely correct in the upholsterer. But Mr Sheridan never did things by halves; and therefore, before the said upholsterer quitted the room he contrived to borrow 200*l*. of him, in addition to the original claim, and he departed, thinking himself highly honoured by Mr Sheridan's condescension in accepting the loan.

I have seen many instances of Mr Sheridan's power of raising money when pushed hard; and one among the rest, I confess even astonished *me*. He was once 3,000*l*. in arrear with the performers of the Italian opera: payment was put off from day to day, and they bore the repeated postponements with Christian patience; but, at last, even their docility revolted, and finding all the tales of Hope flattering, they met, and resolved not to perform any longer until they were paid. As manager, I accordingly received on the Saturday morning their written declaration, that not one of them would appear at night. On getting this, I went to Messrs Morlands' banking-house, in Pall Mall, to request some advances, in order to satisfy the performers for the moment; but, alas! my appeal was vain, and the bankers were inexorable, – they, like the singers, were worn out, and assured me, with a solemn oath, that they would not advance another shilling either to Mr Sheridan or the concern, for that they were already too deep in arrear themselves.

This was a pozer; and with a heart rather sad I went to Hertford

Street, Mayfair, to Mr Sheridan, who at that time had not risen. Having sent him up word of the urgency of my business, after keeping me waiting rather more than two hours in the greatest anxiety, he came out of his bed-room. I told him unless he could raise 3,000*l.* the theatre must be shut up, and he, and all belonging to the establishment, be disgraced.

'Three thousand pounds, Kelly! there is no such sum in nature,' said he, with all the coolness imaginable; nay, more than I could have imagined a man, under such circumstances, capable of. 'Are you an admirer of Shakespeare?'

'To be sure I am,' said I; 'but what has Shakespeare to do with 3,000*l.* or the Italian singers?'

'There is one passage in Shakespeare,' said he, 'which I have always admired particularly; and it is that where Falstaff says, "Master Robert Shallow, I owe you a thousand pounds." – "Yes, Sir John," says Shallow, "which I beg you will let me take home with me." – "That may not so easy be, Master Robert Shallow," replies Falstaff; and so say I unto thee, Master Mick Kelly, to get three thousand pounds may not so easy be.'

'Then, Sir,' said I, 'there is no alternative but closing the Opera House'; and not quite pleased with his apparent carelessness, I was leaving the room, when he bade me stop, ring the bell, and order a hackney-coach. He then sat down, and read the newspaper, perfectly at his ease, while I was in an agony of anxiety. When the coach came, he desired me to get into it, and order the coachman to drive to Morland's, and to Morland's we went; there he got out, and I remained in the carriage in a state of nervous suspense not to be described; but in less than a quarter of an hour, to my joy and surprise, out he came, with 3,000*l.* in bank notes in his hand. By what hocus pocus he got it, I never knew, nor can I imagine even at this moment; but certes he brought it to me, out of the very house where, an hour or two before, the firm had sworn that they would not advance him another sixpence.

He saw, by my countenance, the emotions of surprise and pleasure his appearance, so provided, had excited; and, laughing, bid me take the money to the treasurer, but to be sure to keep enough out of it to buy a barrel of native oysters, which he would come and roast at night, at my house in Suffolk Street. . . .

On my return to town, I told Mr Sheridan what I thought of Dowton; and my opinion being corroborated by George Colman, Dowton had an immediate offer to join the Drury Lane company, which he accepted, and made his first appearance in the same character of Sheva, on the

10th of October, 1796; his success was perfect, and he has continued to this day, a brilliant ornament of his profession.

Mr Sheridan, whose praise in theatrical matters was fame, often told me, that he thought Dowton a sterling actor; and that if he ever wrote a comedy, the two performers for whom he should take most pains, would be Dowton and Jack Johnston – would that he had kept his promise!

Dowton, whom I have proved to be one of the kindest and best-hearted men in existence, was formerly very passionate; and when he believed himself right, nothing could move him from his point. On one occasion, he thought himself slighted, and in a huff, quitted his situation, and retired to the house of his old friend, Mr Lee, of Bexley, a worthy, kind man, whose hospitality is proverbial in the county of Kent.

Mr Sheridan was very sorry to lose so excellent an actor, and wrote to him to return, but all in vain. I went down to Mr Lee's house, at Mr Sheridan's requet, to see what *I* could do, and stopped there two days; but Dowton was inexorable, although every thing he desired would have been granted.

When I returned to town, and told Mr Sheridan of the failure of my mission, he said to me, 'I compare Dowton to a spoiled child at school, who first cries for bread and butter – that is given him; when he has got that, he must have brown sugar put upon it – it is sugared for him; after that, he is not contented till he has glass windows cut out upon it.' However, without having the bread, butter, brown sugar, or glass windows, by the interference of his staunch friend, Cumberland, and the advice of his equally staunch friend, Mr Lee, he returned to his situation; and Sheridan, on the occasion, ordered the revival of two comedies for him, *The Good-natured Man*, and *The Choleric Man*, but (as may be anticipated by those who knew Mr Sheridan) neither of them was ever revived.

At Drury, the next musical piece brought out was *The Honey Moon*, a comic opera, written and composed by Mr William Linley, son of that excellent musician and composer, William Linley, patentee of the Theatre Royal, Drury Lane, and father-in-law to Mr Sheridan. It was produced on the 7th of January, 1797, and reflected great credit on the talents of the author; but owing to an unjust cabal, which was clearly proved to exist on the first night of its performance, it did not meet with that success to which its merits entitled it, and the author (with becoming spirit) withdrew it from the stage. *The Pavilion*, a musical entertainment, written and composed also by Mr William Linley, in which I performed a principal character, was brought out some time after *The Honey Moon*, but did not meet with much greater success, and was also withdrawn for the same reason, though it had some beautiful music in it. The Linley family were all most highly gifted – nature and art combined, did every thing for them. I remember once having the satisfaction of singing a duet with Mrs Sheridan (William Linley's sister), at her house in Bruton Street; her voice, taste, and judgment, united to make her the *rara avis*[1] of her day.

The last time I beheld her heavenly countenance was at Bristol Hot Wells, where she went for the benefit of her health, having been attacked with a severe pulmonary complaint, which baffled every effort of art to overcome it. She was, indeed, what John Wilkes said of her, the most beautiful flower that ever grew in Nature's garden; she breathed her last in the year 1792, in the thirty-eighth year of her age; and was buried by the side of her sister, Mrs Tickell, in the cathedral church of Wells.

Her mother, a kind friendly woman, and in her youth reckoned beautiful, was a native of Wells. Miss Maria Linley, her sister, a delightful singer, died of a brain fever, in her grandfather's house at Bath. After one of the severest paroxysms of the dreadful complaint, she suddenly rose up in her bed, and began the song of, 'I know that my Redeemer liveth', in as full and clear a tone as when in perfect health. This extraordinary circumstance may be depended upon, as my friend, Mr William Linley, her brother, stated the fact to me a short time since.

I never beheld more poignant grief than Mr Sheridan felt for the loss of his beloved wife; and although the world, which knew him only as a public man, will perhaps scarcely credit the fact, I have seen him, night after night, sit and cry like a child, while I sang to him, at his desire, a pathetic little song of my composition, 'They bore her to her grassy grave'. . . .

Superstition often takes possession of the strongest minds. A more powerful instance of the truth of this cannot be cited than that of Mr Sheridan. No mortal ever was more superstitious than he, as I can aver from my own knowledge. No power could prevail upon him to commence any business, or set out upon a journey, on a Friday; nor would he allow, if he possibly could avoid it, a piece to be produced at his theatre on a Friday night. It is a well-known fact (which he never denied), that when Tom Sheridan was under the tuition of Doctor Parr, in Warwickshire, his father dreamt that he fell from a tree in an orchard, and broke his neck. He took alarm, and sent for his boy to London, instanter. The Doctor obeyed the mandate, and brought his pupil to town; and I had the pleasure to meet him at Mr Sheridan's, at dinner. I thought him (though an oddity) very clever and communicative: he was a determined smoker, and, on that day, not a little of a soaker; he drank a great deal of wine, to say nothing of a copious exhibition of hollands and water afterwards.

I remember, when he was asked whom he considered the first Greek scholar in Europe, he answered, 'The first Grecian scholar living is Porson, the third is Dr Burney, – I leave you to guess who is the second.'

On the 13th June, 1808, Madame Catalani performed a scena from *Semiramide*, at Drury Lane Theatre, for my benefit, in which I also performed. On the 17th June, 1808, I played in *No Song, no Supper*, which was my last appearance on the Drury Lane stage, where I had been chiefly the principal male singer for twenty years, but I did not think myself of sufficient consequence to take a formal leave of the public.

I then made an arrangement with Mr Sheridan, to be Musical Director of Drury Lane Theatre, and to continue Stage Manager of the Opera House. While on the stage, I did everything in my power, by persevering industry in my profession, to merit the patronage and liberality which I experienced from an indulgent public. From the first moment I trod the boards of Drury Lane to the moment I quitted it, as far as my feeble efforts went, I endeavoured to support it, through all its perplexities. I had a veneration for the theatre where Garrick and Sheridan had presided, and its best interests were nearest my heart. I felt a proud distinction at having been so fortunate, as for five and twenty years to have enjoyed the most friendly intimacy and unreserved confidence of its highly-gifted proprietor; whom I took upon, take him for all in all, to have been one of the most extraordinary men of the age in which he lived. Mr Sheridan did me the honour (as his friend,) to introduce me to the best society, and the first literary men in the kingdom, who all sought his company. They were sure to find him almost every night at my house, where he was the great magnet of attraction. . . .

On the 24th February, 1809, Mr Richard Wilson gave a dinner to the principal actors and officers of Drury Lane Theatre, at his house in Lincoln's Inn Fields. All was mirth and glee: it was about eleven o'clock when Mr Wilson rose, and drank 'Prosperity and Success to Drury Lane Theatre'; we filled a bumper to the toast; and at the very moment we were raising the glasses to our lips, repeating 'Success to Drury Lane Theatre', in rushed the younger Miss Wilson, now Mrs Montague Oxenden, and screamed out, that 'Drury Lane Theatre was in flames!' We ran into the Square, and saw the dreadful sight; the fire raged with such fury that it perfectly illuminated Lincoln's Inn Fields with the brightness of day. We proceeded to the scene of destruction;

Messrs Peake and Dunn, the treasurers, dashed up stairs, at the hazard of their lives, to the iron chest, in which papers of the greatest consequence were deposited. With the aid of two intrepid firemen they succeeded in getting the chest into the street; – little else was saved.

I had not only the poignant grief of beholding the magnificent structure burning with merciless fury, but of knowing that all the scores of the operas which I had composed for the theatre, the labour of years, were then consuming: it was an appalling sight; and, with a heavy heart, I walked home to Pall Mall.

At the door, I found my servant waiting for me, who told me that two gentlemen had just called, and, finding I was not at home, had said, 'Tell your master, when he comes home, that Drury Lane is now in flames, and that the Opera House shall go next.' I made every effort to trace these obliging personages, but never heard any thing more of them.

Mr Sheridan was in the House of Commons when the dreadful event was made known, and the debate was one in which he was taking a prominent part; in compliment to his feelings, it was moved that the House should adjourn.

Mr Sheridan said, that he gratefully appreciated such a mark of attention, but he would not allow an adjournment, for that 'Public duty ought to precede all private interest'; and with Roman fortitude he remained at his post while his playhouse was burning.

The next morning, several of the principal performers called in Pall-Mall to consider what could be done in the dreadful position of affairs; and while we were debating, a message came from Mr Sheridan, to know where he could meet us? Wroughton, who was at that time our stage-manager, asked John Bannister, Dowton, myself, and a few more of the principal actors, to dine with him in Gower Street; and wrote to Mr Sheridan to request he would meet us there, which he punctually did.

After dinner, lamenting the dreadful situation in which we, as well as himself, were placed by the conflagration, he said, that the first consideration was, to find a place where we could perform, under his 'Drury Lane Patent'; for, though the theatre was destroyed, the patent was not, and that he would make every effort in his power to forward the interests and wishes of the company, without any private consideration of his own, until arrangements might be made to rebuild Drury Lane Theatre. The only request he would make, which was with him a *sine qua non*,[2] was, that the whole of the company, with heart and hand, should stand by one another, and that there should be no separation; 'For', said he, 'I am aware that many of the principal performers may get profitable engagements at the different provincial theatres, but what then would become of the inferior ones, some of whom have large families? Heaven forbid that they should be deserted! – No: I must earnestly recommend and entreat, that every individual belonging to the concern should be taken care of. Let us make a long pull, a strong pull, and a pull altogether; and, above all, make the general good our sole consideration. Elect yourselves into a committee; but keep in your remembrance even the poor sweepers of the stage, who, with their children, must starve, if not protected by your fostering care.'

Such were the sentiments delivered, in my presence, by Mr Sheridan, who, on every occasion which called for the expression of his feeling towards our profession, shewed himself the warmest advocate and supporter of its reputation and prosperity; in confirmation of which, I cannot refrain from quoting the following passage from a letter which he wrote to me some years since, upon my consulting him as to some matters of importance to my professional interests: —

'In my way,' he observes, 'of viewing the profession, and treating its professors, I never considered it fit that the proprietors should, every year, weigh and gauge the decrease of theatrical power which time or accident may have occasioned; and, overlooking past services, hunt, after every change and substitute which may, for the moment, be advantageous.'

This feeling was highly honourable to Mr Sheridan, not only in his character of manager of a theatre, but as indicative of a filial feeling of respect for the profession of which his father had been a member, and by the exercise of which, he had been enabled to give the splendid abilities of his gifted son the advantages of the best cultivation.

NOTES

In 1791, Drury Lane Theatre was reported unsafe and incapable of repair; in 1792, it was pulled down, and Sheridan's company found an expensive temporary retreat first at the Opera House and later at the Haymarket Theatre. The new theatre, rebuilt in 1794, began life with a debt of £70,000. It was Michael Kelly (1764?–1826), the actor, vocalist, and composer, who first introduced to Sheridan's notice the possibilities of filling the treasury by spectacular pieces such as *Cymon*. This piece was produced with due splendour and magnificence, and inaugurated a long line of similar products. Drury Lane, like its master, was thus losing its individual character in an ever-greater tendency towards splendour.

1. A rare bird; prodigy.
2. A necessity; an indispensable condition.

Mr Sheridan*

LORD HENRY BROUGHAM

Thus with an ample share of literary and dramatic reputation, but not certainly of the kind most auspicious for a statesman; with a most slender provision of knowledge at all likely to be useful in political affairs; with a position by birth and profession little suited to command the respect of the most aristocratic country in Europe – the son of an actor, the manager himself of a theatre – he came into that parliament which was enlightened by the vast and various knowledge, as well as fortified and adorned by the more choice literary fame of a Burke, and which owned the sway of consummate orators like Fox and Pitt. His first effort was unambitious, and it was unsuccessful. Aiming at but a low flight, he failed in that humble attempt. An experienced judge, Woodfall,[1] told him 'It would never do'; and counselled him to seek again the more congenial atmosphere of Drury-lane. But he was resolved that it should do: he had taken his part; and, as he felt the matter was in him, he vowed not to desist till 'he had brought it out'. What he wanted in acquired learning, and in natural quickness, he made up by indefatigable industry: within given limits, towards a present object, no labour could daunt him; no man could work for a season with more steady and unwearied application. By constant practice in small matters, or before private committees, by diligent attendance upon all debates, by habitual intercourse with all dealers in political wares, from the chiefs of parties and their more refined coteries to the providers of daily discussion for the public and the chroniclers of parliamentary speeches, he trained himself to a facility of speaking, absolutely essential to all but first-rate genius, and all but necessary even to that; and he acquired what acquaintance with the science of politics he ever possessed, or his speeches ever betrayed. By these steps he rose to the rank of a first-rate speaker, and as great a debater as a want of readiness and need for preparation would permit.

He had some qualities which led him to this rank, and which only required the habit of speech to bring them out into successful exhibition; a warm imagination, though more prone to repeat with variations the combinations of others, or to combine anew their creations, than to

---

* Lord Henry Brougham, *Historical Sketches of Statesmen who Flourished in the Time of George III* (London: Charles Knight, 1839), 1st ser., pp. 211–18.

bring forth original productions; a fierce, dauntless spirit of attack; a familiarity, acquired from his dramatic studies, with the feelings of the heart and the ways to touch its chords; a facility of epigram and point, the yet more direct gift of the same theatrical apprenticeship; an excellent manner, not unconnected with that experience; and a depth of voice which perfectly suited the tone of his declamation, be it invective, or be it descriptive, or be it impassioned. His wit, derived from the same source, or sharpened by the same previous habits, was eminently brilliant, and almost always successful; it was like all his speaking, exceedingly prepared, but it was skilfully introduced and happily applied; and it was well mingled also with humour, occasionally descending to farce. How little it was the inspiration of the moment all men were aware who knew his habits; but a singular proof of this was presented by Mr Moore when he came to write his life; for we there find given to the world, with a frankness which must almost have made their author shake in his grave, the secret note-books of this famous wit; and are thus enabled to trace the jokes, in embryo, with which he had so often made the walls of St Stephen's shake, in a merriment excited by the happy appearance of sudden unpremeditated effusion.

The adroitness with which he turned to account sudden occasions of popular excitement, and often at the expense of the Whig party, generally too indifferent to such advantages, and too insensible to the damage they thus sustained in public estimation, is well known. On the mutiny in the fleet, he was beyond all question right; on the French invasion, and on the attacks upon Napoleon, he was almost as certainly wrong; but these appeals to the people and to the national feelings of the House, tended to make the orator well received, if they added little to the statesman's reputation; and of the latter character he was not ambitious. His most celebrated speech was certainly the one upon the 'Begum Charge' in the proceedings against Hastings; and nothing can exceed the accounts left us of its unprecedented success. Not only the practice then first began, which has gradually increased till it greets every good speech, of cheering, on the speaker resuming his seat, but the minister besought the House to adjourn the decision of the question, as being incapacitated from forming a just judgment under the influence of such powerful eloquence; while all men on all sides vied with each other in extolling so wonderful a performance. Nevertheless, the opinion has now become greatly prevalent, that a portion of this success was owing to the speech having so greatly surpassed all the speaker's former efforts; to the extreme interest of the topics which the subject naturally presented; and to the artist-like elaboration and beautiful delivery of certain fine passages rather than to the merits of the whole. Certain it is, that the repetition of great part of it, presented in the short-hand notes of the speech on the same charge in Westminster Hall, disappoints every reader who has heard of the success which attended the earlier efforts. In truth, Mr Sheridan's taste was very far from being chaste, or even moderately correct; he delighted in gaudy figures; he was attracted by glare; and cared not whether the brilliancy came from tinsel or gold, from broken glass or pure diamond; he overlaid his thoughts with epigrammatic diction; he 'played to the galleries', and indulged them, of course, with an endless succession of clap-traps. His worst passages by far were those which he evidently preferred himself; – full of imagery often far-fetched, oftener gorgeous, and loaded with point that drew the attention of the hearer away from the thoughts to the words; and his best by far were those where he declaimed, with his deep clear voice, though somewhat thick utterance, with a fierce defiance of some adversary, or an unappeasable vengeance against some oppressive act; or reasoned rapidly, in the like tone, upon some plain matter of fact, or exposed as plainly to homely ridicule some puerile sophism; and in all this, his admirable manner was aided by an eye singularly piercing,[2] and a countenance which though coarse, and even in some features gross, was yet animated and expressive, and could easily assume the figure of both rage, and menace, and scorn. The few sentences with which he thrilled the House on the liberty of the press in 1810 were worth, perhaps, more than all his elaborate epigrams and forced flowers on the Begum Charge, or all his denunciatons of Napoleon; 'whose morning orisons and evening prayers are for the conquest of England, whether he bends to the God of Battles or worships the Goddess of Reason';[3] certainly far better than such pictures of his power, as his having 'thrones for his watch-towers, kings for his sentinels, and for the palisades of his castle, sceptres stuck with crowns'.[4] 'Give them', said he in 1810, and in a far higher strain of eloquence, 'a corrupt House of Lords; give them a venal House of Commons; give them a tyrannical Prince; give them a truckling Court, – and let me but have an unfettered press; I will defy them to encroach a hair's-breadth upon the liberties of England'. Of all his speeches there can be little doubt that the most powerful, as the most chaste, was his reply, in 1805, upon the motion which he had made for repealing the Defence Act. Mr Pitt had unwarily thrown out a sneer at his support of Mr Addington, as though it was insidious. Such a stone, cast by a person whose house on that aspect was one pane of glass, could not fail to call down a shower of missiles; and they who witnessed the looks and gestures of the aggressor under the pitiless pelting of the tempest which he had provoked, represent it as certain that there were moments when he intended to fasten a personal quarrel upon the vehement and implacable declaimer.[5]

When the just tribute of extraordinary admiration has been bestowed upon this great orator, the whole of his praise has been exhausted. As a statesman, he is without a place in any class, or of any rank; it would be incorrect and flattering to call him a bad, or a hurtful, or a shortsighted, or a middling statesman; he was no statesman at all. As a party man his character stood lower than it deserved, chiefly from certain personal dislikes towards him; for, with the perhaps doubtful exception of his courting popularity at his party's expense on the two occasions already mentioned, and the much more serious charge against him of betraying his party in the Carlton House negociation of 1812, followed by his extraordinary denial of the facts when he last appeared in Parliament, there can nothing be laid to his charge as inconsistent with the rules of the strictest party duty and honour; although he made as large sacrifices as any unprofessional man ever did to the cause of a long and hopeless Opposition, and was often treated with unmerited coldness and disrespect by his coadjutors. But as a man, his character stood confessedly low; his intemperate habits, and his pecuniary embarrassments, did not merely tend to imprudent conduct, by which himself alone might be the sufferer; they involved his family in the same fate; and they also undermined those principles of honesty which are so seldom found to survive fallen fortunes, and hardly ever can continue the ornament and the stay of ruined circumstances, when the tastes and the propensities engendered in prosperous times survive through the ungenial season of adversity. Over the frailties and even the faults of genius, it is permitted to draw a veil, after marking them as much as the interests of virtue require, in order to warn against the evil example, and preserve the sacred flame bright and pure from such unworthy and unseemly contamination.

NOTES

Lord Henry Brougham (1778–1868), Scottish jurist and political leader. (Editorial matter in square brackets is Brougham's.)
 1. William Woodfall. Sheridan's biographer W. Fraser Rae, however, thinks that it was Sheridan's earlier biographer Thomas Moore who 'propagated the fiction of Sheridan's first speech in the House of Commons being a failure' – Rae, *Sheridan: A Biography*, I, 359n.
 2. ['It had the singularity of never winking'.]
 3. From a speech delivered in 1802.
 4. From a speech delivered in 1807.
 5. [Mr. Sheridan wrote this speech during the debate at a Coffee-house near the Hall, and it is reported most accurately in the Parliamentary debates, apparently from his own notes.]

Recollections of Sheridan*

LORD BYRON

In Byron's Diary for 1813, we read: 'Lord Holland told me a piece of curious sentimentality about Sheridan. The other night we were all delivering our respective and various opinions on him, and mine was this – "Whatever Sheridan has done or chooses to do has been, *par excellence*, the *best* of its kind. He has written the best comedy (*School for Scandal*), the best drama (*The Duenna*, to my mind far beyond that St Giles lampoon, *The Beggar's Opera*), the best farce (*The Critic*, – it is only too good for a farce), and the best address (Monologue on Garrick); and, to crown all, delivered the very best oration (the famous Begum speech) ever conceived or heard in this country." Somebody told Sheridan this the next day, and on hearing it he burst into tears.' 'Poor Brinsley!' adds Byron, 'if they were tears of pleasure, I would rather have said these few but most sincere words than have written the *Iliad* or made his own celebrated Philippic. Nay, his own comedy never gratified one more than to hear that he had derived a moment's gratification from any praise of mine, humble as it must appear to my "elders and betters"' . . . .

'I have more than once heard him say', he writes, '"that he never had a shilling of his own". To be sure he contrived to extract a good many of other people's. In 1815 I had occasion to visit my lawyer in Chancery Lane; he was with Sheridan. After mutual greetings, &c., Sheridan retired first. Before recurring to my own business, I could not help enquiring that of Sheridan. "Oh," replied the attorney, "the usual thing; to stave off an action from his wine merchant, my client." "Well," said I, "and what do you mean to do?" "Nothing at all for the present," said he. "Would you have us to proceed against old Sherry? What would be the use of it?" and here he began laughing, and going over Sheridan's good gifts of conversation. Now, from personal experience, I can vouch that my attorney is by no means the tenderest of men, or particularly accessible to any kind of impression out of the statute or record, and yet Sheridan, in half-an-hour, had found the way to soften

---

* From Thomas Moore, *Life of Byron* (London: John Murray, 1854) pp. 215–16. Editor's title

and seduce him in such a manner that I almost think he would have thrown his client (an honest man, with all the law and some justice on his side) out of the window had he come in at the moment. Such was Sheridan! he could soften the heart of an attorney! There has been nothing like it since the days of Orpheus.'

NOTE

Lord Byron (1788–1824), English poet.

A Dying Man*

GEORGE IV

When I withdrew myself from the opposition, Sheridan certainly became less forward in that party, but not solely out of any deference to me; he had been on bad terms with them from the very formation of their government, and had increased their ill-humour towards him by those sentiments, which he afterwards condensed into the celebrated joke that he had known men knock their heads against walls by accident, but that these Ministers were the first persons he ever had heard of who *built* the wall to knock their heads against. Moreover, Lord [Charles] Grey and Mr [Samuel] Whitbread were become the leaders of the party, and he did not like either; of Mr Whitbread he had an actual hatred; even before Drury Lane affairs had brought them into almost personal conflicts. He therefore naturally, and for every reason, disapproved of Mr Whitbread's taking up the cause of the Princess, and they had warm words about it; and Sheridan always thought that Whitbread wished afterwards to keep him down, and above all out of Parliament, lest he should interfere with the scheme of ambition which he had begun to build on the Princess. I remember Sheridan's telling me with great satisfaction that Whitbread having alluded to Sir John Douglas in some injurious way, Sir John had required an explanation which Whitbread thought fit to make to this officer, who was supposed to be a very determined man, and whose

---

* From *The Croker Papers: The Correspondence and Diaries of the Late John Wilson Croker*, ed. Louis J. Jennings (New York: Charles Scribner's Sons, 1884) I, 279–88. Editor's title.

conduct in the breach of Acre under Sir Sydney Smith has gained him a reputation for courage which Whitbread knew was not to be trifled with.

I don't like mentioning such things, but I must now tell you in confidence that all through our intercourse I had aided Sheridan to an enormous amount. I can venture to say that he has had above 20,000*l*. from me. I gave 1,000*l*. to him the day before he failed.

I need not tell *you* all the circumstances of the last regency question, nor the motives that made me keep my father's Ministers. You knew it all at the time as well as any one. In fact, there was little or nothing, either first or last, that was not pretty publicly known, and I believed printed; at least stated in Parliament. But you recollect the strange figure Sheridan made in the debate when it appeared that he had concealed from his party the fact that my household were ready to resign. This completed the coolness, I might say breach, between them, though he still affected to belong to them.

At last the Parliament was dissolved in, I think, 1812 or 1813,[1] and Sheridan was left without a seat, unless he could get once more returned for Westminster, which there was no chance of, unless he could have the support of the Government. When he mentioned this to me, I saw at once the difficulty of applying the Government interest to the success of a person who had held the principles which Sheridan had formerly professed; but as I knew that he was anything but a Jacobin or democrat, and that in general he agreed in my politics, I thought that if he professed generally Mr Fox's principles, and abstained from pledging himself to the new questions of the day, of which he thought as I did, he might keep most of his old friends; and that friends of the Government might, without inconsistency, prefer him to those who were going great lengths to which it was notorious that Mr Sheridan was really adverse, and would give him their second votes. In truth, I saw no objection to Sheridan and [Lord] Moira's both coming into office, and was desirous that they should do so.

On the subject of the Westminster election I desired Sheridan to see Arbuthnot, who was prepared to give him all the assistance he could on the fair grounds that I had stated.

But Sheridan's natural indolence and procrastination, added perhaps to some feeling that he might risk his popularity, prevented his taking any decisive step. He also had some hopes of Stafford, but there he failed at last, and found himself, as I had feared, out of Parliament, without any chance of getting in.

He came to explain to me his failure at Stafford,[2] of which he had laid all the blame upon Whitbread, of whom he spoke with perfect fury, and called him, I well recollect, *a scoundrel*! He said that Whitbread was already building a scheme of ambition on the Princess; that he was afraid of Sheridan in Parliament on that point; and had determined to keep him out. This induced him, Sheridan said, to refuse to pay him 2,000*l*. which Sheridan had a clear right to, and, as he told me the story, I thought he had.

Some time after this, just before Moira went to India,³ he came to me and said that it was a pity that poor Sheridan at the close of such a life as his had been, should be out of Parliament.

I told him that Sheridan's own indolence and indecision, and his being neither on one side nor the other, were the causes of his being thus left out, but that I had always been ready, and was still, to do all that I could to bring him into Parliament; and *that*, without exacting any dependence on one or any allegiance to the Ministers.

Moira said that he so understood my intentions, or he should not now have approached me with the proposition he had to make, which certainly went rather to place Sheridan again in opposition.

The Duke of Norfolk had a seat to dispose of, for which he expected 4,000*l*., but he consented, as he called it, to subscribe 1,000*l*. towards bringing Sheridan into Parliament; or, in other words, to accept from Sheridan 3,000*l*. for the seat. As even the payment of this sum was not to leave Sheridan perfectly independent, the Duke expecting that he should vote with him, I did not consider the offer quite so noble as the offer of subscribing 1,000*l*. towards bringing Sheridan in seemed to affect to be; but I nevertheless told Moira that I should find some way to get 3,000*l*., and that Sheridan should have it.

This affair, however, did not proceed, from I forget what misunderstanding. Sheridan, however, soon came with a new plan; he had found, he said, a young gentleman who had bought a seat with a right of vacating for another,⁴ and that he had settled with this gentleman (whose name he told us, though I forget) to be elected in his room on payment of the 3,000*l*.

It happened that Moira had 3,000*l*. of MacMahon's⁵ in his hand as a trustee, and it was agreed that this should be advanced to Sheridan, and that Moira and I should be responsible for it, and in the event I had, as might have been expected, to pay the whole sum.

Not that we advanced the sum to Sheridan himself; we knew him too well for that; but the money was lodged in the hands of Mr Cocker, a respectable solicitor named by Sheridan, who was to pay it over to the young man in question when the transfer of the seat should be made. Sheridan took a world of trouble to convince MacMahon that all this transaction was *bonâ fide*. The day before he was to go, he called and took leave of MacMahon, saying he was going to set out early next morning. Late that evening he wrote a note to MacMahon to say that he had forgotten to say something to him, and that as he was to set out at nine next day, he would call in Pall Mall at eight, and begged to have some breakfast. MacMahon laughed at the notion of Sheridan's calling on him at eight; but he came. What he had to say to him I forget, but it ended in urging MacMahon to deposit the money with Mr Cocker, which MacMahon promised should be done. At last Sheridan said 'Come, it is time to be off. My carriage is at the door, and Mr (whatever his name was) is waiting for me.'

I do not know whether by invitation from Sheridan or from some lurking suspicion of his own, but MacMahon walked up with him to where he lived, George Street or Savile Row,[6] or that neighbourhood; where, to be sure, there was a travelling carriage at the door, and servants packing it. Sheridan asked where the horses were. The servants said they were put up till he was ready. 'Very well,' said he, 'put them to as soon as Mr —— arrives.' But Sheridan was quite on the fidget. MacMahon went into the house, and found breakfast laid, and after a little, Sheridan still very fussy; a message came from Mr —— to say that he was detained a few minutes, but would be with him in a quarter of an hour. Then appeared Mrs Sheridan, and MacMahon feeling he was *de trop*,[7] took his leave and left the carriage at the door ready to set off when Mr —— should arrive.

The money, of course, was deposited, and he accepted that Sheridan, as he promised, would write us an account of his reception and his success. The borough, I think, was in Wiltshire, and about eighty or ninety miles from town. Three days after I was on horseback in Oxford Road, and I thought I saw Sheridan at a distance. The person, whoever he was, turned down into Poland Street, or one of those streets, as if to avoid me.

When I came home I sent for MacMahon, and asked him if he had heard of Sheridan. 'No,' said MacMahon, 'not since I saw him *off*', for he had seen him so *nearly off* that he looked on it as the same thing.

'Damn me,' I said, 'if I believe he is gone!' 'Not gone?' 'No. I believe I saw him to-day in town.' 'Impossible!' 'I will not be too confident, but I am almost sure that I saw him in Oxford Road this evening.'

MacMahon was thunderstruck. Next morning, however, came a note to him from Sheridan to say that he was still in town, and would come to explain why, and soon after another note to say that he was coming immediately.

He was this time as good as his word – he came; laid all the blame on the man, Mr ——, whom, however, he only accused of a mistake. He had gone to a coffee house when Sheridan had written to his lodgings, and the note of appointment followed him to his lodgings when he had come back to the coffee house. Sheridan, on the other hand, having written the note which was to say he was waiting for him, thought he might as well look after some business which he had, so he walked out, leaving word that if Mr —— came or sent an answer, it was to be brought to him at Brooks's, or at Drury Lane. If he ever wrote such a note at all, he took good care never to receive any answer; 'but,' he continued to MacMahon, 'all these *malentendus*[8] are rectined, and we are to set out to-morrow at the dawn of day.'

Next day, or the day after, a new note from Sheridan; sorry to say that the negotiations had failed, but he had the pleasure to assure us that a still more satisfactory arrangement was on foot.

MacMahon, however, now became seriously alarmed about the money, and he wrote to Mr Cocker to say that the plan for which the money had been advanced was at an end, and he desired that it might be returned.

Cocker answered that this question of a seat in Parliament was quite new to him; that Mr Sheridan when he desired him to receive the money never hinted at any such object, that it was paid to him on Mr Sheridan's account, and that he had disposed of it according to Mr Sheridan's directions; viz., to pay certain pressing debts, and particularly a debt to himself, Cocker, which he was obliged to press Mr Sheridan for, and which Mr Sheridan directed him to take out of the sum so lodged.

I was, as I told you, obliged to repay this money, but I never saw Sheridan (to speak to) after; not that it was much worse in principle than other things of his, nor that I had given orders to exclude him, but it was felt by Sheridan himself to be so gross a violation of confidence – such a want of respect and such a series of lies and fraud, that he did not venture to approach me, and, in fact, he never came near me again.

He, however, came to MacMahon, and again endeavoured to lay all the blame on Whitbread, who, he said, had got him into all the difficulty; first, by refusing to pay him his 2,000*l*., and afterwards by paying it upon a hard condition which he forced upon Sheridan. 'In short,' said Sheridan, throwing off the air of shame and contrition with which he began the conversation, and taking up a kind of theatrical tone and manner; 'in short,' said he, 'I went to see that scoundrel Whitbread, and it was like the scene at Peachum and Lockit. I told him that I came to tell him that I did not want his assistance, that I retracted the intreaties which my necessities had obliged me to make to him, that I could wait for the 2,000*l*. which he had refused to let me have to get into Parliament, for that I had got 3,000*l*. without being under any obligation to him, and that I should be in Parliament next week. "My dear Sheridan," replied Whitbread, "it is true that I would not give you 2,000*l*. to get into Parliament, and in your circumstances I am sure I acted the part of a true friend, but did I ever refuse you 2,000*l*. *to stay out* of Parliament?" In short, he paid me my 2,000*l*. on condition I should *not come in*, and when I came to ask for the 3,000*l*.

which you, my dear friend, had advanced, for the purpose of returning it to you I found that that fellow Cocker had chosen to apply it to his own debt, and that it was not forthcoming.'

MacMahon listened to all this, but with no good-will towards Sheridan, and came immediately to report it to me, but after that Sheridan never came near either of us.

I sometimes, however, heard of him, and I once saw him by accident, as I shall tell you presently. He now took to live in a very low and obscure way, and all he looked for in the company he kept was brandy and water. He lived a good deal with some low acquaintance he had made – a harness-maker; I forget his name, but he had a house near Leatherhead. In that neighbourhood I saw him for the last time, on the 17th August, 1815. I know the day from this circumstance, that I had gone to pay my brother a visit at Oatlands on his birthday, and next day as I was crossing over to Brighton, I saw in the road near Leatherhead old Sheridan coming along the pathway. I see him now in the black stockings and blue coat with metal buttons. I said to Blomfield, 'There is Sheridan'; but, as I spoke, he turned off into a lane when we were within about thirty yards of him, and walked off without looking behind him. That was the last time I ever saw Sheridan, nor did I hear of or from him for some months, but one morning MacMahon came up to my room, and after a little hesitation and apology for speaking to me about a person who had lately swindled me and him so shamelessly, he told me that Mr Vaughan, Hat Vaughan they used to call him, had called to say that Sheridan was dangerously ill, and really in great distress and want. I think no one who ever knew me will doubt that I immediately said that his illness and want made me forget his faults, and that he must be taken care of, and that any money that was necessary I desired he would immediately advance. He asked me to name a sum, as a general order of that nature was not one on which he would venture to act, and whether *I* named or *he* suggested 500*l*. I do not remember; but I do remember that the 500*l*. was to be advanced at once to Mr Vaughan, and that he was to be told that when that was gone he should have more. I set no limit to the sum, nor did I say nor hear a word about the mode in which it was to be applied, except only that I desired that it should not appear to come from me.

I was induced to this reserve by several reasons. I thought that Sheridan's debts were, as the French say, 'la mer à boire',[9] and unless I was prepared to drink the sea, I had better not be known to interfere, as I should only have brought more pressing embarrassments on him; but I will also confess that I did not know how ill he was, and after the gross fraud he had so lately practised upon me, I was not inclined to forgive and forget so suddenly, and without any colour of apology or explanation; for the pretended explanation to MacMahon was more disrespectful and offensive to me than the original transaction, for he had before told me *why* Whitbread wished to keep him out of Parliament, namely, lest he should serve me in the object nearest my heart, and yet he had suffered Whitbread to bribe him out of my service with his own money, and had then swindled me out of mine.

And, finally, there is not only bad taste but inconvenience in letting it be known what pecuniary favours a person in my situation confers, and I therefore, on a consideration of all these reasons, forbid my name being mentioned at present, but I repeated my directions that he should want for nothing that money could procure him.

MacMahon went down to Mr Vaughan's and told him what I had said, and that he had my directions to place 500*l.* in his hands. Mr Vaughan, with some expression of surprise, declared that no such sum was wanted at present, and it was not without some pressing that he took 200*l.*, and said that if he found it insufficient he would return for more. He did come back, but not for more; for he told MacMahon that he had spent only 130*l.* or 140*l.*, and he gave the most appalling account of the misery which he had relieved with it.

He said that he found him and Mrs Sheridan both in their beds, both apparently dying and both starving. It is stated in Mr Moore's book[10] that Mrs Sheridan attended her husband in his last illness. It is not true; she was too ill to leave her own bed, and was, in fact, already suffering from the disease (cancer of the womb) of which she died in a couple of years after. They had hardly a servant left. Mrs Sheridan's maid she was about to send away, but they could not collect a guinea or two to pay the woman her wages.

When he entered the house he found all the reception rooms bare, and the whole house in a state of filth and stench that was quite intolerable. Sheridan himself he found in a truckle bed in a garret, with a coarse blue and red coverlid, such as one sees used as horsecloths, over him; out of this bed he had not moved for a week, not even for the occasions of nature, and in this state the unhappy man had been allowed to wallow, nor could Vaughan discover that any one had taken any notice of him, except one old female friend – whose name I hardly know whether I am authorised to repeat – Lady Bessborough, who sent 20*l.* Some ice and currant water were sent from Holland House – an odd contribution; for if it was known that he wanted these little matters, which might have been had at the confectioner's, it might have been suspected that he was in want of more essential things.

Yet, notwithstanding all this misery, Sheridan on seeing Mr Vaughan appeared to revive; he said he was quite well, talked of paying off all his debts, and though he had not eaten a morsel for a week, and had not had a morsel to eat, he spoke with a certain degree of alacrity and hope.

Mr Vaughan, however, saw that this was a kind of bravado, and that he was in a fainting state, and he immediately procured him a little spiced wine and toast, which was the first thing (except brandy) that he had tasted for some days.

Mr Vaughan lost no time in next buying a bed and bed clothes, half-a-dozen shirts, some basons, towels, &c., &c. He had Sheridan taken up, and washed, and put into the new bed. He had the rooms cleaned and fumigated. He discharged, I believe, some immediately pressing demands, and, in short, provided as well as circumstances would admit for the ease and comfort, not only of Sheridan, but of Mrs Sheridan also.

I sent the next day (it was not till next day that MacMahon repeated this melancholy history to me) to inquire after Sheridan, and the answer was that he was better, and more comfortable, and I had the satisfaction to think that he wanted nothing that money and the care and kindness of so judicious a friend as Mr Vaughan could procure him; but the next day, that is two days after Mr Vaughan had done all this, and actually expended near 150*l.*, as I have stated, he came to MacMahon with an air of mortification, and stated that he was come to return the 200*l.* 'The 200*l.*,' said MacMahon, with surprise. 'Why you had spent three-fourths of it the day before yesterday!' 'True,' returned Vaughan, 'but some of those who left these poor people in misery have now insisted on their returning this money, which they suspect has come from the Prince. Where they got the money, I know not, but they have given me the amount, with a message that *Mrs* Sheridan's friends had taken care that Mr Sheridan wanted for nothing. I', added Mr Vaughan, 'can only say that this assistance came rather late, for that three days ago I was enabled by His Royal Highness's bounty to relieve him and her from the lowest state of misery and debasement in which I had ever seen human beings.'[11]

NOTES

This narrative concerning Sheridan was dictated to John Wilson Crocker (1780–1857), the British Tory leader and essayist, by King George IV on 26 November 1825.

1. It was in 1812.
2. In October 1812.
3. Lord Moira was appointed Governor-General on 18 December 1812.
4. Mr Attersoll; the borough was Wootton Bassett.
5. Colonel Sir John MacMahon, MP.

6. It was Savile Row.
7. One too many; in the way.
8. Misunderstandings.
9. The sea to drink, i.e. impossibly vast.
10. Moore, *Memoirs of Sheridan*.
11. Sheridan's biographer W. Fraser Rae believes that the King's tale is 'replete with loathsome particulars and it is wholly untrue' – *Sheridan: A Biography*, II, 284.

Remember Me*

He asked what she thought of his looks. She said his eyes were brilliant still. He then made some frightful answer about their being fixed for eternity. He took her hand and gripped it hard, and then he told her that he gave her that token to assure her that, if possible, he would come to her after he was dead, Lady Bessborough was frightened, and said that he had persecuted her all his life, and would now carry his persecution into death. Why should he do so? 'Because,' said Sheridan, 'I am resolved you shall remember me.' He said more frightful things, and she withdrew in great terror.

NOTE

Sheridan always feared death: first as an enemy who could deprive him of those he loved, and later in a more subjective way as well. 'I see a hand you cannot see', he once wrote to his second wife Esther; and now this terror had to be faced. It was a dreadful struggle, and Lady Bessborough had this harrowing story to tell Lord Broughton of the visit she paid Sheridan three days before he died.

---

* From Lord Broughton, *Recollections of a Long Life* (London: John Murray, 1909) II, 102. Editor's title.

Sheridan's Funeral*

LORD BROUGHTON

July 13. – I attended, by desire of the executors, the funeral of this extraordinary man.[1] His remains were removed to the house of Mr Peter Moore,[2] 7, Great George Street, and the attendants walked, two and two, to Westminster Abbey. The procession was headed by the Bishop of London, who had prayed with Sheridan in his last moments, administered the sacrament to him, and spoke of his fervent devotion whilst receiving the sacred elements. The long list of princes, dukes, earls, cabinet ministers, and other personages who followed the coffin to the Abbey is given in Moore's Life of Sheridan.[3] The Burial Service was ill-performed by Dr Fynes, Prebendary of the Cathedral, and no one seemed much affected as the coffin was lowered into the grave, except Mr Charles Sheridan and Mr Linley. The whole ceremony was far less imposing than that which I had witnessed ten years previously when Charles Fox was buried in the Abbey. But, generally speaking, public funerals are not affecting; and often they are very much otherwise – tiresome and scrambling; the beautiful psalms, and even the music, are lost in the length and fatigue of the ceremony.

NOTES

Lord Broughton (1786–1869), English administrator and Liberal pamphleteer.
  1. Sheridan died at 17 Savile Row on 7 July 1816, and was buried in Westminster Abbey on 13 July.
  2. Sheridan's close friend.
  3. 'Seldom has there been such an array of rank as graced this Funeral. The Pall-bearers were the Duke of Bedford, the Earl of Lauderdale, Earl Mulgrave, the Lord Bishop of London, Lord Holland, and Lord Spencer. Among the mourners were His Royal Highness the Duke of York, His Royal Highness the Duke of Sussex, the Duke of Argyle, the Marquisses of Anglesea

* Lord Broughton, *Recollections of a Long Life*, I, 347.

and Tavistock; the Earls of Thanet, Jersey, Harrington, Bessborough, Mexborough, Rosslyn, and Yarmouth; Lords George Cavendish and Robert Spencer; Viscounts Sidmouth, Granville, and Duncannon; Lords Rivers, Erskine, and Lynedoch; the Lord Mayor; Right Hon. G. Canning and W. W. Pole, &c., &c.' – Moore, *Memoirs of Sheridan*, II 315–16.

A Great Man*

GEORGE IV

Sheridan was a great man, but in the simplicity of his nature he never knew his own greatness. His heart was too much enlarged to be governed by his head. He had an abounding confidence in every man; and although his pen indicated a knowledge of human nature, yet that knowledge was confined to his pen alone, for in all his acts he rendered himself the dupe of the fool and designing knave. He was a proud man, sir, a very proud man, with certain conscientious scruples always operating against his own interests. He was a firm and sound adviser; but he was so systematically jealous of his own honour, that he was always willing to grant what he was not willing to accept in return – favours, which might be interpreted as affecting his own independence.

NOTE

The Regent, according to William Earle, remained inaccessible in his closet during the funeral ceremony, and sent for Sheridan's close friend Peter Moore when it was over. He listened to the details of Sheridan's death with the greatest interest, exhibiting a feeling which his interlocutor had never credited him with. Then he spoke these valedictory remarks.

* From [William Earle], *Sheridan and His Times, by an Octagenarian, who Stood by His Knee in Youth and Sat at His Table in Manhood* (London: J. F. Hope, 1859) II, 316–17. Editor's title.

Recollections of Sheridan*

SAMUEL ROGERS

Sheridan, Tickell,[1] and the rest of their set delighted in all sorts of practical jokes. For instance, while they were staying with Mr[2] and Mrs Crewe (at Crewe Hall), Mrs Sheridan and Mrs Crewe would be driving out in the carriage, Sheridan and Tickell[3] riding on before them: suddenly, the ladies would see Sheridan stretched upon the ground, apparently in the agonies of death, and Tickell standing over him in a theatrical attitude of despair. – Again, Mr Crewe expressed a great desire to meet Richardson[4] (author of *The Fugitive*), of whom he had heard Sheridan and Tickell talk with much admiration. 'I have invited him here,' said Sheridan, 'and he will positively be with us tomorrow.' Next day, accordingly, Richardson made his appearance, and horrified the Crewes by the vulgarity and oddness of his manners and language. The fact was, Sheridan had got one of Mr Crewe's tenants to personate Richardson for the occasion. – I don't know whether Richardson's *Fugitive* is a good comedy or not; but I know that Mrs Jordan played very sweetly in it, and that Wewitzer performed a Frenchman most amusingly.

I'll tell you another of Sheridan's youthful pranks. One night, as he, Fitzpatrick, and Lord John Townshend, came out of Drury-lane Theatre, they observed, among the vehicles in waiting, a very handsome phaeton with a groom in it. Sheridan asked the groom to let him get into the phaeton for five minutes, just to try it. The man consented, and stepped down. Sheridan got in, made Fitzpatrick and Townshend get in also, and then drove off at full speed for Vauxhall, whither they were pursued by the groom and a great crowd, shouting and halooing after them. At Vauxhall the groom recovered the phaeton, and was pacified by the present of a few shillings. But it would seem that this exploit had been attended with some unpleasant consequences to Sheridan, for he could not bear any allusion to it: he would say, 'Pray do not mention such an absurd frolic.'

I was present on the second day of Hastings's trial in Westminster Hall; when Sheridan was listened to with such attention that you might have heard a pin drop. – During one of those days, Sheridan, having

* *Recollections of the Table-Talk of Samuel Rogers* (New York: D. Appleton, 1856) pp. 63–71.

observed Gibbon among the audience, took occasion to mention 'the luminous author of *The Decline and Fall*'. After he had finished, one of his friends reproached him with flattering Gibbon. 'Why, what did I say of him?' asked Sheridan – 'You called him the luminous author', &c. – 'Luminous! oh, I meant – *voluminous*.'

Sheridan once said to me, 'When posterity read the speeches of Burke, they will hardly be able to believe that, during his life-time, he was not considered as a first-rate speaker, not even as a second-rate one.'

When the Duke of York was obliged to retreat before the French, Sheridan gave as a toast, 'The Duke of York and his brave followers.'

Sheridan was dining one day at my house when I produced the versified translation of Aristænetus,[5] saying, '*You* are guilty of this.' He made no reply, but took it, and put it, with a smile, into his pocket (from which, of course, I drew it out). What an odd fancy, to turn Aristænetus into verse! Halhed, who assisted Sheridan in that translation, published imitations of Martial, and some of them are very good.

I have seen Sheridan in company with the famous Pamela.[6] She was lovely – quite radiant with beauty; and Sheridan either was, or pretended to be violently in love with her. On one occasion, I remember that he kept labouring the whole evening at a copy of verses in French, which he intended to present to her, every now and then writing down a word or two on a slip of paper with a pencil. The best of it was, that he understood French very imperfectly.

I prefer Sheridan's *Rivals* to his *School for Scandal*: exquisite humour pleases me more than the finest wit.

Sheridan was a great artist: what could be more happy in expression than the last of these lines? you may see it illustrated in the Park every Sunday:

> Hors'd in Cheapside, scarce yet the gayer spark
> Achieves the Sunday triumph of the Park;
> Scarce yet you see him, dreading to be late,
> Scour the New Road and dash through Grosvenor Gate;
> Anxious – yet timorous too – his steed to show,
> The hack Bucephalus of Rotten Row.
> Careless he seems, yet vigilantly sly,
> Woos the stray glance of ladies passing by,
> While his off-heel, insidiously aside,
> *Provokes the caper which he seems to chide.*[7]

I regret that Moore should have printed those memoranda which prove how painfully Sheridan elaborated his compositions; for, though the judicious few will feel that Sheridan was quite right in doing so, the public generally will think the less of him for it. – No wonder that those memoranda were extant: Sheridan was in the habit of putting by, not only all papers written by himself, but all others that came into his hands. Ogle told me that, after his death, he found in his desk sundry unopened letters written by his (Ogle's) mother, who had sent them to Sheridan to be franked.

Sheridan did not display his admirable powers in company till he had been warmed by wine. During the earlier part of dinner he was generally heavy and silent; and I have heard him, when invited to drink a glass of wine, reply, 'No, thank you; I'll take – a little small beer.' After dinner, when he had had a tolerable quantity of wine, he was brilliant indeed. But when he went on swallowing too much, he became downright stupid: and I once, after a dinner-party at the house of Edwards the bookseller in Pall Mall, walked with him to Brooks's,[8] when he had absolutely lost the use of speech.

Sheridan, Sir Walter (then Mr) Scott, and Moore were one day dining with me, and Sheridan was talking in his very best style, when, to my great vexation, Moore (who has that sort of restlessness which never allows him to be happy where he is) suddenly interrupted Sheridan by exclaiming, 'Isn't it time to go to Lydia White's?'[9]

During his last illness, the medical attendants apprehending that they would be obliged to perform an operation on him, asked him 'if he had ever undergone one'. – 'Never,' replied Sheridan, 'except when sitting for my picture, or having my hair cut.'

Sheridan had very fine eyes, and he was not a little vain of them. He said to me on his death-bed, 'Tell Lady Bessborough that my eyes will look up to the coffin-lid as brightly as ever.'

Soon after his death, Lord Holland wrote a short biographical sketch of him, in which it is stated that he showed during the closing scene a deep sense of devotion. But, on my asking the Bishop of London, who had been called in to read prayers to him, what were the religious feelings of Sheridan in his last moments, the answer was, 'I had no means of knowing; for when I read the prayers, he was totally insensible; Mrs Sheridan raising him up, and joining his hands together.'[10]

In his dealings with the world, Sheridan certainly carried the *privileges of genius* as far as they were ever carried by man.

NOTES

Samuel Rogers (1763–1855), English poet.

1. Richard Tickell, who married (1780) Mary Linley, Elizabeth (Eliza) Sheridan's sister.
2. Raised to the peerage (as Lord Crewe) in 1806.
3. Sheridan and Tickell were intimate friends.
4. Joseph Richardson, Sheridan's close friend.
5. Printed, without the translators' names, in 1771.
6. Madame de Genlis's adopted daughter, who was married to Lord Edward Fitzgerald in 1792. According to Madame de Genlis, in her *Memoirs*, two days before she and Pamela left England, Sheridan declared himself, in her presence, the lover of Pamela, who accepted his hand with pleasure; and it was settled that they should be married 'on our return from France, which was expected to take place in a fortnight'. Thomas Moore (*Memoirs of Sheridan*, II, 196) suspects, not without good reason, that in this affair Sheridan was only amusing himself.
7. Prologue to *Pizarro*.
8. Brooks's Club, to which Sheridan was elected on 2 November 1780.
9. Lydia White was a lady who delighted in giving parties to as many celebrated people as she could collect.
10. Cf. 'But the next day he [Sheridan] was not better, and I never saw him. I asked about him, while I sat with Mrs Sheridan; as much, at least, as I thought she chose. I durst not ask much. She told me she had sent for her friend, Dr Howley, then Bishop of London, who had instantly come up from Oxfordshire to pray by him. "And Mr Sheridan," I ventured to say, "what of him?" "I never saw," she replied, "such awe as there was painted in his countenance – I shall never forget it"' – Smyth, *Memoir of Mr Sheridan*, p. 68.

He Beat Them All*

LORD BYRON

I do not know any good model for a life of Sheridan but that of Savage.[1] Recollect, however, that the life of such a man may be made far more amusing than if he had been a Wilberforce; – and this without offending the living, or insulting the dead. The Whigs abused him;[2] however, he never left them. As for his creditors, remember, Sheridan never had a shilling and was thrown, with great powers and passions, into the thick of the world, and placed upon the pinnacle of success, with no other external means to support him in his election. Did Fox pay his debts? – or did Sheridan take a subscription? Was the **'s drunkenness more excusable than his? Were his intrigues more notorious than those of

---

* Lord Byron, *Letters and Journals*, ed. Rowland E. Protheroe (London: John Murray, 1898–1901) IV, 239. Editor's title.

all his contemporaries? and is his memory to be blasted, and theirs respected? Don't let yourself be led away by clamour but compare him with the coalitioner Fox, and the pensioner Burke as a man of principle, and with ten hundred thousand in personal views, and with none in talent, for he beat them all *out* and *out*. Without means, without connexion, without character (which might be false at first, and make him mad afterwards from desperation) he beat them all, in all he ever attempted. In writing the Life of Sheridan, never mind the angry lies of the humbug Whigs. Recollect that he was an Irishman and a clever fellow, and that *we* have had some very pleasant days with him.

NOTES

Before Sheridan's second wife Esther died, she asked Thomas Moore to write her husband's life. Moore asked Lord Byron, the poet, for suggestions, and received this good down-to-earth advice.
  1. Richard Savage (1697–1743), playwright and poet. Dr Samuel Johnson in his life of Savage says, 'This was the golden part of Mr Savage's life, his appearance was splendid, his expenses large, and his acquaintance extensive.' Savage was noted for his charm and witty conversation, but eventually died in penury. Sheridan wrote a prologue to Savage's play *Sir Thomas Overbury* when it was produced at Drury Lane Theatre.
  2. In Sheridan the Whig Party acquired a new Member who proved his usefulness by hard work on the matter of Bills and by persuasive wit and skill in debate.

More Recollections of Sheridan*

LORD BYRON

'Lewis[1] was not a very successful writer. His *Monk* was abused furiously by Mathias, in his *Pursuits of Literature*, and he was forced to suppress it. *Abellino* he merely translated. *Pizarro* was a sore subject with him, and no wonder that he winced at the name. Sheridan, who was not very scrupulous about applying to himself *literary* property at least,

* Thomas Medwin, *Conversations of Lord Byron: Noted During a Residence with His Lordship at Pisa* (London: Henry Colburn, 1824) pp. 233–5. Editor's title.

manufactured his play without so much as an acknowledgment, pecuniary or otherwise, from Lewis's ideas;[2] and bad as *Pizarro* is, I know (from having been on the Drury-Lane Committee, and knowing, consequently, the comparative profits of plays,) that it brought in more money than any other play has ever done, or perhaps ever will do.

'But to return to Lewis. He was even worse treated about *The Castle Spectre*, which had also an immense run, a prodigious success. Sheridan never gave him any of its profits either. One day Lewis being in company with him, said, – "Sheridan, I will make you a large bet." Sheridan, who was always ready to make a wager, (however he might find it inconvenient to pay it if lost,) asked eagerly what bet? "All the profits of my *Castle Spectre*," replied Lewis. "I will tell you what," said Sheridan, (who never found his match at repartee,) "I will make you a very small one, – what it is worth." '[3]

I asked him if he had known Sheridan?

'Yes,' said he. 'Sheridan was an extraordinary compound of contradictions, and Moore will be much puzzled in reconciling them for the Life he is writing. The upper part of Sheridan's face was that of a god – a forehead most expansive, an eye of peculiar brilliancy and fire; but below he shewed the satyr.'

NOTES

1. Matthew Gregory Lewis (1775–1818), English novelist, dramatist and poet; nicknamed 'Monk' after his Gothic novel *The Monk*.
2. *Pizarro* was Sheridan's adaptation of a literal translation of August von Kotzebue's *The Spaniards in Peru*.
3. *The Castle Spectre*, produced on 14 December 1797, had a prodigious run, owing partly to the 'sublime effect' of the sinking of the Ghost in a flame of fire and in 'beautiful Gothic scenery'. It was acted forty-six times, and Sheridan did not pay the author his dues. The case was carried into court, where Sheridan savagely attacked Lewis. Their enmity persisted until the year of Sheridan's death.

In Defence of Sheridan*
ALICIA LEFANU

It now only remains to examine some passages relating to the late Right Hon. Richard Brinsley Sheridan himself.

The first is a literary mistake. It is observed in the *Memoirs*,[1] p. 182, 183.

'When the breathings of affection are expressed in harmonious numbers, and clothed with the richness of metaphor, they are certain of giving pleasure to the female object of adoration. Even the extravagance of hyperbolical adulation, and the absurdity of allegorical comparison, will, in such cases, be received as pure incense, of which these lines descriptive of the personal charms of Miss Linley afford a striking evidence:

> 'Mark'd you her eye, &c.'

Now it so happens that the lines by R. B. Sheridan, beginning, 'Mark'd you her eye', were written in praise, not of Miss Linley, but of Lady Margaret Fordyce, sister of Lady Anne Lindsay, the charming author of 'Auld Robin Gray', and at that time the reigning belle of Bath. An anonymous poem, entitled, 'The Bath Picture', had appeared, containing a description of the principal beauties then admired at that fashionable watering-place. When the bard arrived at the name of Lady Margaret Fordyce, he could only afford her the following moderate praise:

> Remark too the dimpling sweet smile
> Lady Margaret's fair countenance wears.

Mr Sheridan, who was often of Lady Margaret's parties, and felt for her the enthusiastic admiration of a young poet, seized the pen, and in an answer to 'The Bath Picture', entitled, 'Clio's Protest, or The Picture Varnished', after several pretty severe strictures on other parts of the poem, thus castigates the anonymous bard for his insensibility, and vindicates the lady's transcendant charms:

---

* From *Memoirs of the Life and Writings of Mrs Frances Sheridan* (London: G. and W. B. Whittaker, 1824) pp. 392–435. Editor's title.

> But hark! did not our bard repeat
> The love-born name of Margaret?
> Attention seizes every ear;
> We pant for the *description* here.
> If ever dulness left thy brow,
> Pindar, we say, 'twill leave thee now.
> But oh! old Dulness' son anointed,
> His mother never disappointed;
> For after all we're left to seek
> A *dimple* in Fordyce's cheek.
> And could you really discover,
> In gazing those sweet beauties over,
> No other charm, no winning grace,
> Adorning either mind or face,
> *But one poor dimple* to express
> The quintessence of loveliness.
> Mark'd you her eye of sparkling blue?
> Mark'd you her check of rosy hue?
> That eye in liquid circles moving;
> That cheek abash'd at man's approving;
> The one, Love's arrows darting round,
> The other blushing for the wound;
> Did she not speak, did she not move,
> Now Pallas, now the Queen of Love!

 The reader of taste will perceive a great beauty in the sudden change of accent in the line beginning, 'Mark'd you her eye', which actually gives the impression that the poet had struck into a new measure, although the poem is throughout in eight syllable verse.

 The last eight lines were set to music, and became deservedly popular. They breathe the very soul and spirit of beauty, and flow with a force and fire which proves how successfully Mr Sheridan might have devoted himself to poetry, had not higher cares entirely absorbed his attention.

 I shall not offer any more poetical extracts, not to trench upon the claims of another publication; but *this one* was necessary to show, that if the Biographer of Mr Sheridan had read but a few lines more, he could never have made the mistake of applying these verses to Mrs Sheridan, as he would have seen both the name of 'Margaret' and of 'Fordyce' inserted. As for the rest of the paragraph, granting the assertion upon which it is grounded to have been correct, the expression, 'the extravagance of hyperbolical adulation', is misplaced: because, however inapplicable to Mrs Sheridan's *peculiar* style of beauty the praise contained in the above lines might be, her claim to universal admiration, not only for personal charms, but for talent, taste, judgement, and excellence of disposition, placed her so high in the opinion of all who knew her, as to make it much more difficult to find expressions adequate to her merit, than to risk falling into enthusiastic praise.

The next passage I shall proceed to notice, occurs in pages 193–4–5, in which the long-contested question is debated, whether Mr Sheridan should have let his wife sing in public or not? a question in which the biographer considering him as 'a man possessing neither pedigree nor property', p. 195, throws his weight into the scale in favour of the measure. I know that nothing is so likely to excite the ridicule of the superficial, as an attempt to vindicate family pretensions: yet, at the hazard of encountering it, I must repel the first part of this unfounded assertion. If an unbroken descent from a family of equal antiquity and respectability in Ireland; a family which made its rare boast that none of its descendants of either sex had ever transgressed the laws of honour, and which, though at the beginning of the last century it no longer possessed the large estates that the ancient geographers of the kingdom assigned to the Sheridans, yet never fell from its rank among the respectable gentry of the county of Cavan – If this does not constitute a 'pedigree' honourable, though not ennobled, I am unacquainted with the meaning of the term.

The learned and conscientious prelate William Sheridan, Bishop of Kilmore and Ardagh, who held that united see in the reign of Charles the Second, and was deprived for refusing to take the oaths at the Revolution, was not, as Dr Watkins supposes (p. 2), a distant relation of the Sheridan family. The grandfather of Dr Thomas Sheridan was younger brother of the Bishop of Kilmore. Perhaps it was the beauty of the alliteration 'Pedigree and Property' in the preceding paragraph, that tempted the biographer, who thus continues:

'He carried his high notions so far, *as to prevent his wife* from singing at a royal concert, alleging that such an exhibition would degrade his character as a gentleman.' – P. 193.

This is an unfortunate mistake. The biographer had heard *something about* a royal concert, but totally mistook the circumstances. The fact was, that Mr R. B. Sheridan's objections were conquered in this one instance; and he unhesitatingly *gave his consent* that his wife should sing at the royal concert; the elevated character of that entertainment having obviated his former objections, Mrs Sheridan was to have appeared there, when an unexpected change in the arrangements for the royal amusements, into which it is unnecessary to enter more particularly in this place, occasioned the idea to be given up.

Dr Watkins goes on:

'It was observed, and justly, that Sheridan having no property of his own, *nor any calling by which he could maintain a family*, exerted an arbitrary authority in restraining his wife from following the occupation to which she had been bred, and by which she could not fail in a few years to realize a fortune.'

Now Mr Sheridan was at this time a member of the Middle Temple; and, had not more tempting (perhaps not more fortunate) prospects opened to his view, he had as fair a promise of advancement in his profession as the most brilliant and astonishing talents could afford. His wife also was in no immediate distress; as the most highly gifted of his daughters, she was always distinguished by her father's favour, and had made enough by her professional exertions before marriage as to render the continuance of them unnecessary. But Dr Watkins thinks they owed their existence at that time to the Magazines.

'But he still continued inflexible, though it was with great difficulty he could raise the necessary supplies, *and that by very equivocal means*. One of his resources was that of writing for the fugitive publications of the day, in which he was materially assisted by his wife.

'He has been heard to say, "Mrs Sheridan and myself were often obliged to keep writing for our daily leg or shoulder of mutton, otherwise we should have had no dinner." One of his friends to whom he confessed this, wittily replied, "Then I perceive it was a *joint concern*"'

At the hazard of demolishing a story so facetious, we must take leave to assure the biographer, that wherever he picked up that Joe Miller, it can bear no reference to Mr and Mrs Sheridan. Highly gifted and accomplished as was the latter, she never aspired to the honours of authorship; and the very time fixed upon as the period of these obscure literary exertions was much passed by the young couple in different visits at the country houses of friends no less distinguished for virtue than for the high rank they held in society; – friends, who delighted in the extraordinary combination of merit and agreeable qualities that Richard Brinsley Sheridan and his beautiful wife displayed; but who would assuredly not have continued to value him if he had been the character here represented; providing, '*by very equivocal means*', for an inglorious existence.

Before we dismiss the subject of *music*, it is with pain that justice compels the notice of another instance of misrepresentation.

'Though he (R. B. Sheridan) continued to reject all the overtures that were made for the public appearance of his wife, he readily suffered her to have private concerts, if they could properly be so denominated, by which it was probable more was obtained than could have been received in the display of her skill and melody in places of general admission.

'*Thus the same thing was practiced with a finer name*; for whatever distinction an air of fashion might have given to these concerts, *the subscription by which they were supported was in reality the price given for an entertainment.* The income thus obtained at London and Bath was very handsome.' – P. 196.

In all and every particular of this statement the biographer was misinformed. Mr and Mrs Sheridan gave some private concerts at their house in Orchard-street, Portman-square, as a return for the civilities and hospitality they received from many persons of fashion and consequence. A music-room was accidentally annexed to their house, and it was the least expensive entertainment they could give; the performers consisting entirely of Mrs Sheridan's family. Never, surely could the lovers of music have received a more exquisite gratification than that which was afforded on these occasions by the combined talents of Mrs Sheridan, her father, her sisters, Mary and Maria, and her brother, Thomas Linley. But these concerts were, as I have already said, given as the discharge of a debt of civility already incurred. No money was ever received, nor were any such concerts given at Bath.

Richard Brinsley Sheridan and his wife certainly were in straitened circumstances, but he extricated himself by his own exertions. The comedy of *The Rivals*, which met with great and deserved success, was succeeded by the opera of *The Duenna*, which had a run never equalled in the annals of dramatic history but by that of *The Beggar's Opera*. His profit was proportionably great, and the early display of such talent seemed to point out to him a never-failing resource.

Yet while *The Duenna* was in rehearsal at Covent Garden, Barry[2] (then in his decline,) expressed to the elder Mr Sheridan his opinion that it would not succeed; and gave as his reason, 'That there was too much *church music* in it'; by which singular expression he meant the slow and solemn airs, 'Oft does Hymen', 'O had my love', 'Gentle Maid', 'What Bard, O Time', and others.

The event shewed that Barry was no prophet; and two years afterwards, *The School for Scandal* placed Mr Sheridan at the summit of theatrical celebrity. On this Dr Watkins observes, some people were of opinion that the comedy 'was not the performance of Sheridan; *by some it was attributed to the pen of Mrs Sheridan*'. – P. 218.

With regard to Mrs Sheridan's authorship, I have given a satisfactory answer in another place; but here comes a more alarming accusation.

'There were persons who roundly asserted *that the play was written by a young lady, the daughter of a merchant in Thames Street*; that at the beginning of the season, when Mr Sheridan commenced his management, the MS. was put into his hands for his judgment; soon after which the fair writer, who was then in a state of decline, went to Bristol Hot-wells, where she died.

'*Very observable* it is, that notwithstanding the general circulation of a charge, which, if true, must materially injure the moral and literary reputation of Sheridan, he never took the pains of repelling it, or of establishing his right to the brightest performance that bears his name.' – P. 221. He never took the pains of repelling a report that his play was written by a *young* lady! *The School for Scandal*, by a *young lady, the daughter of a merchant in Thames Street!!!*

But lest it should be said that exclamation is not argument, and that one single fact is worth the most eloquent expressions of indignation, I will here briefly give the history of *The School for Scandal*, upon the undoubted authority of the author's only surviving sister;[3] and thus oppose to the groundless calumny that clear refutation which Mr Sheridan through his life disdained to give.

Early introduced into the world, and placed in difficult and critical situation, Mr R. B. Sheridan often saw his own name the sport of calumny, which, although it sometimes excited a smile, yet often gave rise to more painful feelings. At Bath, then famous for the manufacture and circulation of ungrounded stories, his duels and other romantic adventures were magnified and misrepresented in a thousand different ways. When he was recovering of his wounds, it was one of his amusements to read the daily accounts of himself in the papers and say, 'Let me see what they report of me to-day; I wish to know whether I am dead or alive', &c. (The ridiculous and contradictory reports then afloat, certainly gave rise to the highly humourous duel scenes in *The Rivals* and *The School for Scandal*.) Other falsehoods sunk deeper into his heart; and having a mind turned to reflection, although his spirits were often led away by gaiety, the young poet conceived the noble plan of attacking the 'Hydra, scandal, in his den', and exposing, in a spirited picture, the wide extended mischief that may ensue from the encouragement of a censorious spirit.

His sister, who was with him when these ideas were first working in his mind, had the opportunity of watching his thoughts as they arose, while yet they were 'Like diamonds in their infant dew'.

His biographer says, –

'The moral tendency of *The School for Scandal*, is the part upon which its greatest admirers will find it difficult to say any thing conclusive or satisfactory.'

Certainly, those who seek for morality in the character of Charles Surface, will be disappointed, but if they look for the moral tendency of *The School for Scandal* in the proper place, it will be found to be excellent. In Mr Sheridan's play the faulty character of the piece is one common to the drama, though rendered partly original by the spirit, generosity and feeling, which the writer added from himself. The moral portion, on the contrary, is his own, and is conceived in a manner equally just, pointed, and forcible. It consists in a lively exposure of the effects of a baneful propensity, in which many scruple not to indulge, who would shrink from the imputation of any other failing, –

a propensity to slander and detraction. It points out to decided, though not to equal abhorrence, the dark and insidious plotter against reputation, the feeble and deceitful defender, the bitter and malignant censurer, and the good-humoured but thoughtless retailer of the envenomed lie. *These* are chastised, perhaps reformed, by the characters of Lady Sneerwell, Mrs Candour, Sir Benjamin Backbite, and Lady Teazle; and are taught to fear at least the shafts of ridicule, when to their hardened minds the moralist or the preacher might address themselves in vain.

For what I have further to say upon the subject I shall avail myself of his sister's own words, without whose sanction my remarks could have no authority; and as the suspicions thrown out about *The School for Scandal* have perhaps had some effect, it is trusted the answer will be read with candour and attention.

'The whole story of the supposed manner in which the play of *The School for Scandal* came into Mr Sheridan's hands is perfectly groundless, the writer of these lines having frequently heard him speak on the subject long before the play appeared; many of the characters and incidents related to persons known to them both, and were laughingly talked over with his family.'

It is particularly remembered that, in the first sketch, the character which now bears the name of Mrs Candour, went by that of Lady Kitty Candour: a title which, I presume, Mr Sheridan abandoned on account of its too great resemblance to one in a dramatic piece of Foote's – Lady Kitty Crocodile; which was supposed to be meant for the Duchess of Kingston. Before he put pen to paper, the fable, as perfectly conceived and matured in his mind, was communicated to his friends; and the expression he made use of, described at once the completeness and unity of his plan. – 'The comedy is finished; *I have now nothing to do but to write it.*' This mode of composition is probably the only one in which the author can hope to give to his works the impression of energy and correctness.

The biographer continues:

'It certainly is *not a little extraordinary*, that while the other dramatic pieces of Mr Sheridan have been committed to the press by his authority, and for his emolument, that which exceeds them all, and has brought most honour to his name, still remains unpublished', &c. – P. 218.

'When such stories were afloat, *the obvious course* pointed out by prudence and justice, was that of publishing the play.' – P. 220.

'This was not done, and the seclusion of the piece within the walls of the theatre, together with a total forbearance of all explanation on the part of the manager, served to strengthen the suspicion that, *however embellished* the tale might be, it was not altogether fiction.' – P. 221.

In making these remarks, the biographer seems to have forgot the nature of theatrical literary property, or he would have perceived it was *not at all extraordinary* that *The School for Scandal* should not have been published till the period of literary property was expired. *It was not published, because* Mr Sheridan chose to confine the performance of the play in London to his own theatre. Once a play is printed, such a monopoly can no longer be enjoyed. If he therefore wished to profit by the fruits of his own labours, it was by no means to be expected of 'Prudence', that she should point it out as his *obvious course* to print his play, and thereby give Mr Harris, of Covent Garden, an equal right to have it performed at his theatre.[4] *The Duenna*, on the contrary, was not printed because the copyright was disposed of to Mr Harris at the time it appeared. The Comedy of *The Rivals*, was published during the run of the play. As Dr Watkins is very fond of quoting the opinion of Dr Johnson, whenever his opinion is inimical to the Sheridan family, we beg leave to remind him that Johnson, in recommending R. B. Sheridan for a member of the Literary Club, mentioned him particularly as the author of the best modern Comedy; without deigning to make the least reference to the absurd and ridiculous calumnies *said* to be even then already in circulation.

That Mr Sheridan should have stopped just as his muse gave so rich a promise, must have been regretted by many, as well as by the noble bard who so elegantly eulogized his memory, and who thus apostrophized him while living;

> Oh, SHERIDAN! if aught can move thy pen,
> Let Comedy resume her throne again;
> Give, as thy last memorial to the age,
> One classic drama, and reform the stage.

But, from a different cause, complete success sometimes produces the same effect as discouragement, in preventing an author from venturing again. Mrs [Elizabeth] Inchbald, in her 'Remarks' upon the different reception of Gay's *Beggars' Opera*, and *Polly*, observes, that an unsuccessful author ought to continue to write, and may perhaps write himself into reputation; but, that a perfectly successful one had better lay down his pen, lest a sudden blight should fall upon his laurels. It may be further observed, that from this time forward, Mr Sheridan was thrown into the busy vortex of public life, and engaged in a distracting multiplicity of affairs, such as has perhaps seldom fallen to the lot of one individual. The time necessary for polishing and bringing works of fancy to perfection was absolutely denied him: and a laudable jealousy of his literary reputation may be allowed in the man, who, not long after his death, was concisely, but aptly characterized by an eminent living tragedian, as having 'written the best comedy that ever was acted, and spoken the best speech that ever was spoken'.

Before I dismiss the subject of the drama, I must notice the biographer's conjecture:

'When it is considered Mr Wallis was the confidential agent of Mr Garrick, and that Mr Ford stood on terms of the greatest intimacy with him, some foundation is afforded to substantiate what was said at the time, that Mr Sheridan was indebted to the generosity of his friend and predecessor, Garrick, for the interest which he obtained in the concern of Drury Lane', &c. To which it is only necessary to answer, that there is *no foundation* for the assertion. Neither Mr Sheridan nor his father ever had the least pecuniary obligation to Garrick whatsoever.

Equally erroneous are the statements respecting the Linley family.

'In *quick succession* she (Mrs Sheridan) lost two accomplished brothers.' – P. 316.

Further on, it is said:

'Thomas, the celebrated composer and performer on the violin, *was carried off in a few days by a raging fever*. Another fine youth, named Samuel, *was accidentally drowned in a pond*. Maria, who had been the delight of the lovers of harmony by her extraordinary vocal powers, expired *at the harpsichord*, while singing the praises of her Redeemer.

'The remembrance of his unmarried daughter (Maria), whose musical talents were the theme of universal admiration, never failed (with Mr Linley) to open the bleeding wounds inflicted *by the awful manner of her dissolution.*'

'Mr Linley, in fact, never recovered from the effects of this last heavy blow (the death of Mrs Sheridan); which hurried him to the grave, leaving a widow and *one son* to lament', &c. – *Memoirs of the public and private Life of the Rt Hon. R. B. Sheridan.*

In these three paragraphs there are four mistatements. It was Mr Thomas Linley, Mrs Sheridan's eldest brother (and *not* Samuel, as stated in the *Memoirs*) who was unfortunately drowned, while amusing himself in a pleasure boat, at the seat of the Duke of Ancaster, in the year 1778. He was *one* year younger than Mrs Sheridan (not *seven years*, as stated in the *Memoirs*, P. 128). Mr Thomas Linley was a young man of great merit, and uncommon musical abilities. A *few years afterwards*, his younger brother, Samuel, a lieutenant in the navy, was cut off by a fever. In the year 1785, Miss Maria Linley died at Bath, of a fever. So that it appears, between the death of Thomas and Maria Linley, there was an interval of *seven* years; a space of time which hardly justifies the expression in the *Memoirs*, (P. 316) that Mrs Sheridan had '*scarcely* poured forth her sorrows' over the untimely graves of her brothers, 'before she was called upon to lament the death of her favourite sister, who expired at Bath on the fifth of September 1784, while singing Handel's exquisite and soul-enlivening anthem, "I know that my Redeemer liveth".

The extraordinary story of Miss Maria Linley's 'expiring at the harpsichord', is not correct. She died, as has been already stated, of a fever; and was attended by Dr Harrington, a gentleman no less celebrated for his medical skill than for his musical abilities. A little time previous to her death, when confined to her bed, she raised herself up, and with unexpected and momentary animation sung a part of the anthem, 'I know that my Redeemer liveth'. The female attendant, who related the scene to Mrs H. Lefanu[5] (the mother of the writer), described it as the most affecting she had ever witnessed. The pathetic, and almost super-human sweetness of the notes breathed by the young and lovely creature, who was just departing from them, and the awful hope inculcated in the words of the air she had chosen, contributed to give an appearance of inspiration to this last effort of a voice that had delighted every ear. Dr Harrington was greatly overcome by the scene, and could only exclaim, 'She is an angel!' as he left the room. Exhausted by the effort, she sunk into the arms of her attendant, and shortly afterwards breathed her last.

In the year 1787, Mrs Sheridan experienced a still greater affliction in the death of Mrs Tickell, the sister nearest to her in age, and the chosen friend of her heart.

The mention of Mrs Tickell naturally leads to the notice of a ludicrous mistake, though one of small importance, that occurs in Dr Watkin's *Memoirs*, on the subject of Mr Tickell's second marriage.

'Not long after the death of his first wife, Mr Tickell married Miss Leigh, *who is mentioned so respectfully in the preceding letter*, and who deserved his esteem by her accomplishments and virtues. She was the daughter of a Commander in the Marine Service of the East-India Company.'

Here *two* very different ladies are manifestly blended into one: for the lady 'so respectfully mentioned in the letter', was Miss Sophia Lee, of Belvedere House, Bath, author of *Canterbury Tales*, &c. under whose care Miss Tickell was placed, and who never was married. The beautiful Miss Leigh, whom Mr Tickell took for his second wife, as the reader will observe, spelt her name differently.

The statement respecting Mr Linley's surviving family is not more correct than the preceding one. He left *three* children; two sons, William Linley, Esq., the Rev. Ozias Linley, and a daughter, Jane, afterwards married to the late Charles Ward, Esq., Secretary to the Committee of Management of the Theatre Royal Drury Lane.

The following mis-statement, however, is an error of greater magnitude; and as it materially affects the late Rt Hon. R. B. Sheridan, the writer will be excused for dwelling more at length upon it, than on the preceding. It relates to the death of the first Mrs Sheridan, at Bristol.

'One morning, when Mrs Sheridan was about to take an airing on the neighbouring downs, she found that the carriage and horses had just been taken in execution by an unfeeling creditor. It may naturally be supposed that a shock so sudden and rude would operate with deadly effect upon a frame already enfeebled beyond the power of recovery, and hanging as it were by an imperceptible thread over the margin of the grave. The stroke, indeed, acted with similar violence to the wintry blast upon a tender plant; for the sufferer, bending before it, burst into tears, and retired into her chamber, out of which she never came again till the lifeless form was conveyed to the silent mansion, "*where the wicked cease from troubling, and where the weary are at rest*".' – (*Memoirs of the Right Hon. R. B. Sheridan.*)

It is not clear *who* is meant by the concluding quotation in the text, but the biographer may rest assured, that, through whatever channel he obtained the anecdote of the carriage being stopped, it is quite an invention. Had such a circumstance taken place, Mrs Sheridan was surrounded by tender and watchful friends, who never would have exposed her to the *chance* of such a shock. The fact was, she was with great difficulty conveyed to Bristol, and never regained strength to bear the motion of a carriage. She ventured a few times to the Wells in a sedan chair, her husband walking beside her. Indeed, the affection and solicitude he shewed during the whole time of her illness, was such as could not be surpassed.

A lady of the highest respectability, whose friendship for Richard Brinsley Sheridan and his wife was of twenty years' standing, and who was with Mr and Mrs Sheridan at the time of her decease, thus wrote to Mrs H. Lefanu, who was in Ireland, and most anxious to know every particular respecting a friend so dear.

'............ The truth is, our poor friend is in a most precarious state of health, and quite given over by the faculty. Her physician here, who is esteemed very skilful in consumptive cases, assured me from the first it was a *lost case*; but as your brother seemed unwilling to know the truth, he was not so explicit to him, and only represented her as being in a very critical situation. Poor man! he cannot bear to think her in danger himself, or that any one else should, though he is as attentive and watchful as if he expected every moment to be her last. It is impossible for any man to behave with greater tenderness, or to feel more on such an occasion than he does.'

If these expressions do not contradict the charge of thoughtless unkindness on Mr Sheridan's part, which must be inferred from the anecdote in the text, I know of none sufficiently strong to answer that purpose. The description of Mrs Sheridan's death-bed scene is still more striking.[6]. . .

A few days after the funeral, Mr Sheridan removed to a house he had at Isleworth, where he remained, 'with no other companions but his two children', in whom his heart was at that time entirely wrapped up. The little girl[7] whom Mrs Sheridan had left in infancy, was represented by all who saw her to have possessed a surprising degree of beauty: she was in fact the miniature of her mother; but, as might be expected under the circumstances of her birth, small and delicate, and giving very little expectation of long life. This uncommon resemblance to her mother endeared the infant beyond expression to her afflicted parent, who could not bear her a moment out of his sight. He was dreadfully agitated on his arrival at Isleworth, and though he constrained himself to appear cheerful in the presence of others, all his solitary hours were given up to the anguish of sorrow and regret; still, for the sake of his son Thomas, who behaved to his father with constant and tender attention, but whose young mind required a change from the constant contemplation of melancholy objects, Mr Sheridan resolved to make an effort, and in the beginning of August after his irreparable loss, he entertained a few intimate friends on a visit of a week at Isleworth. The following is a description of his deportment.

'We never saw him do the honour of his house before; that, you know, he always left to that dear, elegant creature, who never failed to please and charm every one who ever came within the sphere of her notice. Nobody could have filled her place so well; he seemed to have pleasure in making much of those whom she loved, and who, he knew, sincerely loved her. We all thought he never appeared to so much advantage. He was attentive to every body and every thing, though grave and thoughtful; and his feelings, poor fellow, often ready to break forth in spite of his efforts to suppress them. He spent his evenings mostly by himself.'

Towards the end of October Mr Sheridan took a house at Wanstead. He had his son Thomas there with his tutor, Mr Smyth, and had removed his nursery to it about a year, when, at a little evening entertainment, given chiefly to the young friends of his son, his feelings were destined to be shocked by the most dreadful domestic misfortune that could befal him, – the death of his infant daughter Mary. . . .

It remains now only to notice a few particulars erroneously stated in his biography, relative to his elder brother the late Mr Charles Francis Sheridan, p. 463. He is said to have been 'in principle quite the reverse of his brother, who never lived with him on good terms'.

This is not correct. Mr Charles Francis Sheridan was by no means the reverse of his brother in political principles, though from his early connexions he generally acted with government. Neither is it at all true that the brothers were not on good terms; as it was during the shortlived Rockingham Administration, in which Richard Brinsley Sheridan was under Secretary of State, that he obtained for his brother the place of Secretary at War, (*not* under Secretary of State for the War department, as mentioned by Dr Watkins,) in Ireland. The residence of the brothers in different kingdoms prevented their intercourse from being frequent; but when Mr Charles Francis Sheridan visited England, a short time before his death, the intercourse between him and his brother was perfectly friendly and cordial. Their opinions in many points coincided; for the talents of Charles Francis Sheridan were great as well as those of his brother. He was originally intended for the diplomatic line, in which it was a pity he did not continue, as no man was more formed by nature and education for success in it; possessing as he did the French language, (the universal language of courts,) in its utmost elegance and perfection, to which he joined an engaging suavity of manners, totally divested of the usual self-importance of office. On his return from Sweden, where at the early age of twenty he enjoyed the confidential situation of Secretary to the British Embassy, Mr Charles Francis Sheridan wrote an account of the celebrated revolution, for which he was furnished with the most ample and valuable materials by the Ambassador, Sir John Goodricke himself. Of the eagerness with which this work was received, Boswell gives the following amusing account. 'At Mr Dilly's to-day, were Mrs Knowles, (the ingenious quaker lady,) Miss Seward, the Rev. Dr Mayo, and the Rev. Mr Beresford. Before dinner Dr Johnson seized upon Mr Charles Sheridan's *Account of the late Revolution in Sweden*, and seemed to read it ravenously, as if he devoured it, which was to all appearance his method of studying. "He knows how to read better than any one", said Mrs Knowles; "he gets at the substance of a book directly; he tears out the heart of it." He kept it wrapt up in the tablecloth in his lap during the time of dinner, from an avidity to have one entertainment in readiness when he should have finished another: resembling (if I may use so coarse a simile) a dog who holds a bone in his paws in reserve, while he eats something else which has been thrown to him.'

After his return from Sweden, Mr Charles Francis Sheridan was entered a student at the Temple, and was called to the Bar in Ireland about the year 1779. A violent fever that endangered his life, and left great remains of weakness, induced him to give up the active part of the profession; and he studied that branch of the law called special pleading. His appointment of Secretary at War in Ireland, obliged him to give up this respectable and lucrative branch of the law. Charles Francis Sheridan was member of Parliament for the borough of Belturbet, county of Cavan; and (from his office) a Privy Counsellor. Besides the *History of the Revolution of Sweden*, he was the author of a very celebrated tract upon Poyning's Law, and of several other valuable legal pamphlets. At his death[8] he left a widow very amply provided for, three daughters, and two sons. In the *Memoirs of the Right Honourable Richard Brinsley Sheridan* it is erroneously stated that they both 'died in the East, where they filled situations of trust', &c. – P. 463. Charles, the eldest, held a place under government in Ireland, and died in that country a few years after his father. Thomas, the youngest son, was sent to India as a writer; he was a young man of merit in every respect, and high in the esteem of his superiors, when he was carried off by a fever at Shiraz, in Persia, a short time after his going abroad.

Richard, the son of the elder Mr T. Sheridan's brother, a barrister of high reputation, and King's counsel, represented the borough of Charlemont, in Ireland, having been called to that situation of trust by the late excellent Earl of Charlemont, solely in consequence of the high esteem that nobleman entertained for his character.[9]

With respect to the elucidations in justification of certain passages of the late Richard Brinsley Sheridan's private life, I do not pretend to give any thing from myself, but write them as furnished to me from documents of the highest authority and respectability. They will not be deemed impertinent or misplaced, when his near relationship is considered to the amiable woman[10] whose life forms the chief subject of these *Memoirs*: a woman whose time was devoted to the duties of domestic life, and the education of her children; a mother, whose distinguished talents and fond endearments were remembered and regretted by Mr Sheridan, even in the meridian of his own fame and distinction; and who, could she look down from the place which we humbly trust her well-spent life must assign her, could not be supposed to consider the highest worldly success as a compensation for her son's having deservedly incurred the charge of neglecting every virtue.

NOTES

Alicia Lefanu was Sheridan's niece.

1. John Watkins, *Memoirs of the Public and Private Life of R. B. Sheridan, with a Particular Account of His Family and Connexions*, 2 vols (London: Henry Colburn, 1817). This is the first of Sheridan's biographies, published the year following his death.
2. Spranger Barry, the actor.
3. Elizabeth (Betsy) (1758–1837).

4. 'When the lapse of time gave to Covent Garden and other theatres the right of representing *The School for Scandal*, Mr Sheridan had thoughts of publishing it along with other plays, to which he meant to have prefixed prefaces: and it is certainly to be regretted that his various avocations prevented the execution of this plan, which would probably have presented the public with a valuable body of dramatic criticism' – Alicia Lefanu.
5. Sheridan's sister Elizabeth married Henry Lafanu in 1789.
6. For a description of Elizageth Sheridan's deathbed in this book see 'An Agonising Scene', p. 55.
7. Mary, who was born on 30 March 1792 and died on 23 October the following year.
8. In 1806.
9. See Francis Hardy, *Memoirs of the Political and Private Life of J. Caulfield, Earl of Claremont* (London: privately printed, 1810) II, 318.
10. Frances Sheridan, Sheridan's mother.

Mr Sheridan*

CHARLES BUTLER

It gives the Reminiscent great pleasure to perceive, that Mr Moore's interesting biography of Mr Sheridan,[1] has confirmed the account given of the eloquence of that extraordinary man in the preceding volume of *Reminiscences*. His public life may be divided into four states, successively commencing with, his attracting the notice of the public by *The Duenna*; – his coming into Parliament; – the part which he took during the king's first malady; – and his conduct in the settlement of the Regency at the close of the late reign.

The natural turn of Mr Sheridan's mind, led him rather to covet eminence, as a monarch's favourite, or as one pre-eminently shining in a brilliant court, than in fulminating a popular assembly, and wielding the democratic.[2] But his supreme ambition was, to be thought the best possible manager of a theatre. When fortune placed Lord Erskine at the English bar, she perhaps fixed him in the only station in which he could elevate himself to fame and fortune: when she placed Mr Sheridan in the management of a theatre, she fixed him in a situation which delighted him, but for the filling of which with honour or advantage, he was totally unqualified. The Reminiscent has often seen him, in moments of better recollection, when unfortunately the *jucundissima recordatio vitæ bene actæ*[3] was wanting to him: his regret in

* Charles Butler, *Reminiscences* (Boston, Mass.: Wells and Lilly, 1827) pp. 86–97.

those hours was, not at his failure of success in his political career, but at his not having devoted himself to the Muses. He used to say that he was designed for poetry; for the *forte epos*.[4] But never was a man less qualified for any literary exertion, which required grandeur or simplicity.

> Mark, how the dread *Pantheon* stands!
> Amid the domes of modern hands,
> Amid the idle toils of state;
> How simply, how severely great!
>
> Akenside.

No compositions are less formed than those of Mr Sheridan, to be compared with the character of the Pantheon: but some 'domes of modern hands, some idle toils of state', are exquisitely pretty and brilliant. With the best of these, some compositions of Mr Sheridan may be justly thought to bear an analogy. The Reminiscent once read to Mr Sheridan the finest specimen of his poetry, his *Epilogue to Semiramis*. 'O! why did I not,' he exclaimed, 'uniformly addict myself to poetry; for *that* I was designed!' 'But then,' said the Reminiscent, 'would you have been the admiration of the senate? Would London have emptied itself to hear your phillippic on Mr Hastings? Would you have been the intimate of Mr Fox? Would you have been received, as doing honour to it, at Devonshire-house?' – 'What,' he replied, 'has all this done for me? What am I the better for the admiration of the senate, for Mr Fox, for Devonshire-house? I have thrown myself away. But you shall see to-morrow.'

> 'To-morrow and to-morrow,'
>
> Shakespear.

his friend naturally replied.

It was a general subject of wonder, that, as he had shewn how well he could write for the stage, he should write so little. 'The reason is,' said Mr Kelly, with exquisite felicity, 'that Mr Sheridan is afraid of the author of *The School for Scandal*.'

Mr Sheridan's bon mots were not numerous; but when he was in good humour, the subject pleased him, and he liked his company, he sometimes displayed a kind of serious and elegant playfulness, not apparently rising to wit, but unobservedly saturated with it, which was unspeakably pleasing. Every thing he then said or did, was what delights Englishmen so much, and what they understand so well – in the style and manner of a perfect gentleman.

Occasionally, however, he had brilliant sallies. On one occasion he and the late Mr Sheldon, of Weston in Warwickshire, supped with the Reminiscent. Mr Sheldon was born of Catholic parents, and brought up a Catholic; he embraced the Protestant religion, and sate in two parliaments. The Catholic question being mentioned, Mr Sheridan, supposing Mr Sheldon to be a Catholic, told him, 'he was quite disgusted at the pitiful, lowly manner in which Catholics brought forward their case: Why should not you, Mr. Sheldon, walk into our house, and say, – "Here am I, Sheldon of Weston, entitled by birth and fortune to be among you: but, because I am a Catholic, you shut your door against me."' 'I beg your pardon,' said Mr Sheldon, interrupting him, 'I thought it the duty of a subject to be of the religion of his country; and therefore – ' 'You quitted,' said Mr Sheridan, interrupting him, 'the errors of popery, and became a member of a church which you know to be free from error? I am glad of it; you do us great honour.' The subject then changed; but it was evident that Mr Sheldon did not sit quite easy. At length, the third of the morning hours arrived; Mr Sheldon took his watch from his pocket, and holding it forth to Mr Sheridan, 'See,' he said to him, 'what the hour is: you know our host is a very early riser.' 'Damn your *apostate watch*!' exclaimed Mr Sheridan; 'put it into your Protestant fob.'

It has not, I think, been mentioned by any of his biographers; but the fact certainly is, that Mr Sheridan was very superstitious, a believer in dreams and omens. One sentiment of true religion the Reminiscent has often heard him express, with evident satisfaction; that in all his writings, and even in his freest moments, a single irreligious opinion or word had never escaped him.

Frequently, he instantaneously disarmed those who approached him with the extreme of savageness, and a determined resolution to insult him. He had purchased an estate, at Surrey, of Sir William Geary, and neglected to pay for it. Sir William mentioned this circumstance to the Reminiscent; and the English language has not an expression of abuse or opprobrium, which Sir William did not apply to Sheridan. He then marched off, in a passion; but had not walked ten paces, before he met Mr Sheridan. The Reminiscent expected as furious an onset as 'if two planets should rush to combat';[5] but nothing like this took place. In ten minutes Sir William returned, exclaiming, 'Mr Sheridan is the finest fellow I ever met with; I will teaze him no more for money.'

Lord Derby once applied, in the Green Room, to Mr Sheridan, with much dignity, for the arrears of Lady Derby's salary, and vowed he would not stir from the room till it was paid. 'My dear Lord,' said Mr. Sheridan, 'this is too bad; you have taken from us the brightest jewel in the world; and you now quarrel with us for a little dust she has left behind her.'

Politics was not a favourite subject with Mr Sheridan. Though he always voted for Catholic emancipation, it was observed that, when the question was before the House, he did not speak for it: and that, even in common conversation, he expressed himself with much less feeling than might have been expected. Some, from whom a contrary conduct was expected, embraced Mr Perceval's anti-catholic system; others, among whom was Mr Sheridan, avoided declaring against it. 'But you may be assured,' Mr Sheridan said to an Irish Catholic gentleman of distinction, 'that though we don't shew it, our hearts are with you.' 'And you also,' replied the gentleman of Ireland, 'may be equally well assured, that if the French should land in Ireland, though we should not join you, our hearts will be with you.'

It was evident to all, who lived with Mr Sheridan, that, a *jalousie d'amitié* between him and Mr Burke, subsisted long before the debates during the late Kings's first malady, – when, for the first time, it was *generally* perceived. It was suspected that Mr Sheridan's favouritism at Carlton House, was not pleasing either to Mr. Burke, or to Mr Burke's great friend. It is clear that Mr Fox was, for some time before his decease, completely estranged from him.

From this time, Mr Sheridan appeared a faded man. His pecuniary embarrassments thickened upon him; his usual expedients for removing them began to fail him, and in all places, and in all hours, he was too soon and too completely overpowered by the conqueror of *Ariadne*.[6] Cardinal de Retz[7] relates in his memoirs, that, during the troubles at Paris, in consequence of the war of the Fronde, *Henrietta, the grand- daughter of Henry IV. of France*, and the wife of our Charles I., who, with her children, had fled from England, and then resided in that city, was reduced to such a state of misery, that, in a severe January, she was without wood, or coals, or money to procure them; and that her daughter Henrietta Maria, afterwards the wife of the Duke of Orleans, the brother of Lewis XIV., was obliged to remain in bed to preserve herself from the cold.

At times, Mr Sheridan's abode was in an equal state of want.

Mr Sheridan's affectionate and respectful regard for the memory of his first wife was great, and pleasingly discovered itself on numerous occasions. Notwithstanding the many unpleasant scenes in his latter life, it was evident to all who saw them, that Mr Sheridan and his second wife were warmly attached to each other. Nothing could be more edifying or more elegant, than the behaviour of Mr Sheridan and, – the hare with many friends, – his son by his first wife, to each other.

Reflections have been cast on some friends of Mr Sheridan, for their alleged insensibility to his distresses. But his previous usage of them should be taken into account. None, but those, who witnessed it, can conceive, the repeated instances of unfeeling and contumelious disregard, which he shewed them, by his total want of punctuality in his engagements, and his heedlessness of the inconveniences and losses, which it occasioned them. One of the most remarkable of these provoking and distressing scenes was exhibited by him, in the last election, which took place, in his life-time, for the town of Stafford. The late Mr Edward Jerningham, whose family had a strong interest with the electors, exerted himself to the utmost, as did the most illustrious person in the kingdom, to rouse Mr Sheridan to proper activity on an occasion, which evidently was of so much importance to him; and on which his liberty and independence seemed to depend.

All was vain: – he did not leave London, till it was almost impossible he should reach Stafford, in time to make an effective canvass. When he reached it, he loitered inactive at the inn, the mob all the while calling clamorously for him. The consequence was, that he lost his election. But such was the fascination of his manner, and such the attraction of his name, that, before he left the town, the electors seemed to be in despair that they had not voted for him, and a large proportion of them would escort him out of the town. All that has been said of the zeal displayed by an illustrious person, for Mr Sheridan's success, on this occasion, was confirmed, by the account given of it to the Reminiscent, by Mr Edward Jerningham, an eye-witness of all that passed in it, either in London or Stafford.

Perhaps Mr Sheridan's most splendid exhibition was his speech in the court of Chancery, at the hearing of the cause upon the bill filed against him by the trustees of Drury-lane Theatre. The court was crowded; Mr Sheridan spoke during two hours, with amazing shrewdness of observation, force of argument, and splendour of eloquence: and as he spoke, from strong feeling, he introduced little of the wit and prettyness, with which his oratorical displays were generally filled. He was heard with great attention and interest: while his speech lasted, a pin might be heard to drop. But it did not prevent Mr Mansfield from making a most powerful reply. He exposed, in the strongest terms, the irregularity of Mr Sheridan's conduct as manager of the theatre; and the injuries done by it to the proprietors, creditors and performers. Upon these, Mr Mansfield commented in the bitterest terms; and every word he said sunk deep into Mr Sheridan's heart. The Chancellor appeared to pity the calamities of a man so talented and so abusing his talents. He finished his discourse, by conjuring Mr Sheridan to think seriously of the words, with which Dr Johnson concludes his life of Savage, – that 'those, who, in confidence of superior capacities or attainments, disregard the common maxims of life, will be reminded, that nothing will supply the want of prudence; and that negligence and irregularity long continued, will make knowledge useless, wit ridiculous, and genius contemptible'.

Most anxious was Mr Sheridan to procure from Mr Mansfield, something that had an appearance of a retraction of the charges which he had brought against him. To obtain this, he made many direct and many indirect efforts. All he could obtain from Mr Mansfield was a declaration, at a consultation with the Reminiscent, at which Mr Sheridan was present, that 'he spoke from the affidavits in the cause; so that his assertions and arguments depended, for their justice, on the truth of the facts mentioned in those'. This was little: but it comforted Mr Sheridan much.

We have mentioned the four divisions of Mr Sheridan's life: the brilliant portion of it was that, which intervened between his election to parliament and Mr [Spencer] Perceval's triumph over the Fox and Grenville administration. During this period, Mr Sheridan's irregularities and pecuniary distresses were at times very great, still The *Duenna, The School for Scandal*, and his parliamentary fame shed a lustre round him, and buoyed him up against the waves, which threatened him, and by which he was afterwards overwhelmed. But, from the time, we have mentioned, his supports began to fail him, and ultimately left him to want and poignant regret. Few, even of those, who were absolute strangers to Mr Sheridan, have read the last pages of Mr Moore's Biography of him, without pain; few have not wished, that some pages of a certain review of that work had not been written.

NOTES

Charles Butler (1750–1832), English writer on legal and theological subjects.
1. Moore, *Memories of Sheridan.*
2. Alludes to Milton.
3. Most joyful recollection of a life well lived.
4. Heroic epic.
5. Milton, *Paradise Lost*, VI.313–15.
6. Ariadne was the daughter of King Minos of Crete. She fell in love with the Athenian youth Theseus, gave him a sword and the thread to carry by which he found his way back out of the Labyrinth wherein he slew the Minotaur.
7. Cardinal de Retz (1614–79), French ecclesiastic and politician.

The Character of Sheridan*

WILLIAM CULLEN BRYANT

It was the misfortune of Sheridan that his animal nature, if we may so speak, had so much the mastery over his intellectual. He not only loved pleasure with a more impetuous fondness, but suffered less from the excessive pursuit of it than most men. The strength of his constitution, the possession of high health, the excitability of his feelings, and his fine flow of animal spirits, all either seconded the temptations of the siren, or secured him from the immediate penalties which so often follow her gifts. In proportion to his love of pleasure was his hatred of labor. No man loves labor for its own sake – at least not until long habit has made it necessary – but some seem originally to dread and hate it more vehemently than others. It is almost impossible to imagine anybody more unwilling to look this severe step-mother of greatness and virtue in the face than was Sheridan. This disposition showed itself while he was yet a school-boy, and seems to have lost no strength in his maturer years. He never had, he never would have, any regular pursuit, for neither his connection with the theatre nor his parliamentary career deserve this name. He avoided all periodical industry; it was a principle of his conduct to delay everything to the last possible moment; and his whole life seems to have been a series of experiments to escape, or at least to put off to another day, that greatest of evils – labor. Yet he was capable, in a high degree, of intellectual exertion; and the instances in which he submitted himself to it are so many successful experiments of the force of his genius. His political career was marked by the same unpersevering character as his private life. He was ambitious but his was not that deep-seated ambition which broods long over its plans, and follows and watches them, year after year, with unexhausted patience. If a single blow could prostrate the party he opposed, Sheridan was the man to strike it – and with great force; but it was not for him to assail it with attacks, continually repeated, till it was overthrown. After a powerful effort, he would turn again to his pleasures and dissipations until they palled upon him, or until the entreaties of friendship, or some sudden excitement of feeling, recalled him to the warfare. That such a man should, notwithstanding, have

* From a review of Moore's *Memoirs of Sheridan*, *New York Review*, 2 (Feb 1826) 165–81; repr. in *Prose Writings of William Cullen Bryant*, ed. Parke Godwin (New York: A. Appleton, 1884) II, 366–9.

exerted himself so far as to produce those celebrated comedies and speeches which were the admiration of his age, may be easily accounted for on these views of his character. His indolence was not of that dreamy kind which delights in visions of its own creation; no man was less imaginative than Sheridan. It is true that there are some attempts at fancy in his writings, but they do not seem to be the natural effusions of his mind. They were evidently written for display, and consist of broken images laboriously brought together. Indeed, it would probably have been fortunate for him had he delighted more in reveries of the imagination, for it is the tendency of these to make us look with a kind of dissatisfaction on the world about us; but it was the error and the danger of Sheridan that he loved that world, and its splendors and its pleasures, quite too well. He was not disposed to search for imaginary enjoyments, but to possess himself greedily and immoderately of those within his reach. He was the creature of society; its light and changing excitements were the food of his mind; and to dazzle and astonish it was a pleasure which he enjoyed with the highest zest. This is the secret of those irregular and brief, but for the time vigorous, sallies of industry. Everything with him was planned for effect; his comedies, his operas, his speeches, are all brilliant, showy, and taking. His more elaborate efforts, however, were stimulated by the additional motive of necessity. *The Rivals* and *The Duenna* were written when he was forced to think of doing something for a livelihood, and *The School for Scandal* at the same period. All his exertions respected some immediate advantage. He loved to shine, but thought not of laying up fame for future ages; just as he loved the enjoyments of wealth, but chose not to perplex himself for its accumulation and preservation. It was characteristic of Sheridan that he was too economical of labor even to labor in vain. All the quips and jests and smart things which came into his head he treasured up for the convivial meeting or the floor of Parliament. He came fresh from his stolen studies, on subjects of which he was before ignorant, to make a splendid speech about them before the vividness of his new impressions had faded from his mind. Among the few papers left behind him, it would seem, from the extracts given us by Mr Moore, that there was nothing on which much study had been expended, nor which was in itself capable of being made valuable.

Sheridan was a man of quick but not deep feelings; of sudden but not lasting excitements. He was not one of those who suffer a single passion to influence the whole course of their lives. Even the desire to dazzle by his wit, great as was its power over him, was not always awake, for we are told that he would sometimes remain silent for hours in company, too lazy to invent a smart saying for the occasion, but idly waiting for the opportunity to apply some brilliant witticism already in his memory. His writings themselves show that he never dwelt long enough on any particular feeling to analyze it; the few attempts at sentimentalism they contain are excessively false and affected; their excellence lies wholly in a different way. His romantic love for the beautiful, amiable, and accomplished woman who became his wife, though his biographer would have us believe that it continued unabated to the end of her life, seems to have operated on his mind only at intervals, for it is hinted in this very book that it was not steady enough to secure his fidelity. Her death, and that of her little daughter, who soon followed her, deeply as they affected him at the time, threw no cloud over his after-life. His griefs might have been violent, but they were certainly brief, and he quickly forgot them when he came to look again at the sunny side of things. Even his political disappointments do not seem in the least to have soured his temper, or abated his readiness to adopt new hopes and new expedients. Indeed, it seems not improbable, from some appearances of pliancy in his political character, that, had not his daily habits enfeebled the vigor of his mind and shortened a life which great robustness of constitution seemed to have marked out for a late old age, he might have long continued a favorite with the present sovereign of England.

Some of the excellences of Sheridan's character were such as could not easily suffer by this disposition to indolence and pleasure. That a man possessing an abundant flow of agreeable animal sensations, determined to make a matter of enjoyment of everything, and to avoid everything in the shape of care, should have possessed likewise an engaging good nature, is by no means extraordinary. That he who had no solitary pleasures, but whose happiness was in some way connected with that of those about him, should be obliging, generous, and humane, is almost a natural consequence. The man who lives only among and by his friends is naturally led to study the art of making friendships. Nor is the frankness and openness of Sheridan's disposition any less in harmony with the rest of his character. It is not among men of his temperament that we are to look for the habit of dissimulation, for concealed designs, and the weaving and carrying on of frauds and artifices. The labor and perplexity of falsehood were with him sufficient objection, had no other existed, to the practice of it. The anxious and persevering necessity to provide against detection he left to those who were more steadily diligent than himself. Had the practice of deceit been as easy as that of integrity, we are not sure that Sheridan would not have fallen into it, induced by the prospect of immediate and present advantages which it always holds out – for it seems that he had not sufficient firmness of principle to resist the temptations of many other vices.

NOTE

William Cullen Bryant (1794–1879), American poet and editor.

The Real Sheridan*

THE MARQUIS OF DUFFERIN AND AVA

No man has ever lived in more worlds than Sheridan, or has ever shone with such brilliancy in all. In the world of fashion, in the company of wits, among authors, painters and poets, in the House of Commons, at the Court of the Prince Regent, – whatever society he frequented, – he moved a star. His charming manners, his handsome person, his gaiety, and, above all, his good nature, which was one of his principal characteristics, rendered him universally popular. But these engaging qualities were sometimes marred by the foibles and peculiarities which are most apt to attract attention and to serve as weapons in the hands of a man's enemies. In early manhood he became one of the chiefs of a political party when party strife ran high, and when virulent calumny and abuse, in an age more coarse than ours, were considered legitimate means of offence, and his memory has suffered accordingly. Moreover, from his youth, two impediments clogged and embarrassed his every step, – his poverty and his Irish origin.

Sober English common-sense has always been suspicious of impecunious brilliancy in public men. While admiring, it distrusts it. Talent, to command confidence, especially in those days, had to be supplemented by wealth or birth; otherwise it was regarded as consisting, like a comet, of shining and attenuated gases, and its possessor was dubbed 'an adventure'. Now, Sheridan was not only poor but improvident, and though few could have been better born, so far as good birth is dependent upon ancient ancestry and feudal distinction in a man's own land, he had no root in the country of his adoption. This latter circumstance was almost an insuperable bar to political advancement. The chief offices of the State were then regarded as the patrimony of the great Whig and Tory families, to which it would be presumption for a stranger to aspire. But, although Sheridan forced his way through this artificial barrier and was soon associated in a close confederacy with Fox and the other Whig leaders, the straitened circumstances of

---

* From Rae, *Sheridan: A Biography*, I, viii–xii. Editor's title.

his youth, in spite of the large though precarious income subsequently created by his talents, dimmed his prestige, embarrassed his daily life, and enveloped his declining years in disheartening gloom. Yet, notwithstanding the burning of Drury Lane Theatre, his debts in their totality were never considerable, and at his death did not much exceed £5,000. Though owing little, however, he owed that little to a great number of people, who were themselves needy, and who filled heaven and earth with their complaints. Had Sheridan, like Fox, Pitt, Burke and many a contemporary, owed vast sums of money to persons of his own degree, we should have heard little of these obligations; but to withhold £5, justly due to your bootmaker, is properly considered more discreditable than an indefinite tardiness in repaying £10,000 to a too-confiding friend.

For a like reason Sheridan's conviviality has been more rigorously denounced than many a contemporary toper's sodden and unredeemed intemperance. Wine quickly disordered his high-strung nervous system; and, while delighting the harder-headed drinkers around him with the sallies of his wit, two or three glasses were sufficient to overset the delicate poise of his brain. As a consequence, his cheerful and comparatively innocent indiscretions over the bottle have been more frequently in men's mouths than the results of deeper potations of his more stolid boon companions. In later life, alas! for a certain period, grief and accumulated misfortunes drove him into more serious lapses, but from the dominion of these, to his great credit be it said, he eventually redeemed himself.

From the foregoing it will, I think, be easily understood how it came about that an altogether mythical Sheridan should have been presented to the imagination of the present generation, and how idle fables and a thousand trivial and sometimes disparaging anecdotes should have accumulated by the force of attraction round an individuality so various in its moods, so many-sided, so dramatic, and so eminently social. Even Moore, his contemporary, with every means of information at his disposal, was obliged to admit, when concluding his biography, that he really knew little about Sheridan; while, in the opinion of another authority, 'the real Sheridan has disappeared for ever'.

NOTE

The Marquis of Dufferin and Ava was Sheridan's great-grandson. After he had read and admired W. Fraser Rae's *Wilkes, Sheridan, Fox: The Opposition under George III*, he suggested to its author that he should undertake a complete biography of Sheridan.

Bibliography

This bibliography includes the principal accounts of the life of Sheridan, plus some additional material not represented in this book.

'Anecdote of Sheridan', *Port Folio*, 5th ser., 5 (May 1818) 395 [a comical story of Sheridan, which has not been asserted as a fact].

'Anecdote of Sheridan', *The Times*, 24 Sep 1842, p. 5 [Sheridan used to say that the life of a manager was 'a constant superintendence of executions'].

Ayling, Stanley, *A Portrait of Sheridan* (London: Constable, 1985).

Baker, H. Barton, 'Richard Brinsley Sheridan', *Gentleman's Magazine*, 2nd ser., 21 (Sept 1878) 304–20.

Beaver, Alfred, 'The Beautiful Sheridans', *Longman's Magazine*, 45 (Nov 1904) 70–9 [Tom Sheridan and his three daughters Helen Selina, Caroline Elizabeth Sarah, and Georgiana].

Bingham, Madeleine, *Sheridan: The Track of a Comet* (London: Allen and Unwin; New York: St Martin's Press, 1972) [provides an extended biography].

Black, Clementina, *The Linleys of Bath* (London: Martin Secker, 1911; rev. edn London: Miller, 1971) [provides an account of the courtship and marriage of Sheridan and Elizabeth Linley].

Boaden, James, *Memoirs of Mrs Siddon* (Philadelphia: H. C. Carey and I. & L. Lea; New York: G. & C. Carvill, 1827) [recollections by the famous English actress].

Boomsliter, Paul C., 'The Parliamentary Speaking of Richard Brinsley Sheridan' (PhD dissertation, University of Wisconsin, 1942).

Bor, Margot, and Lamond Clelland, *Still the Lark: A Biography of Elizabeth Linley* (London: Merlin Press, 1962) [recounts the life of Sheridan's first wife].

Butler, E[liza] M., *Sheridan: A Ghost Story* (London: Constable, 1931) [surveys Sheridan's life as well as previous biographies of him].

Byron, Lord, 'Extracts of a Monody to the Memory of the Late Right Hon. R. B. Sheridan, Recited at the Opening of Drury-Lane Theatre, Sep 7, 1816', *Gentleman's Magazine*, 86 (Oct 1816) 350.

Copeland, Lewis (ed.), 'At the Trial of Warren Hastings', *World's Great Speeches*, 2nd rev. edn (New York: Dover, 1958) pp. 165–8 [prints the peroration (the last ten paragraphs) of Sheridan's Westminster Hall speech against Hastings (13 June 1788)].

Darlington, W. A., *Sheridan*, Great Lives series, no. 15 (London: Duckworth, 1933) [recounts Sheridan's life with an effort to be objective].

——, *Sheridan*, Bibliographical Supplement to *British Book News* (London: Longmans, 1951) [organises a sketch of Sheridan's life and career].

Devonshire, Georgiana, Duchess of, 'Georgiana, Duchess of Devonshire's Diary', in Sichel, *Sheridan, from New and Original Material*, II, 399–426 [shows how Sheridan was the Prince's right-hand man in all the negotiations during the First Regency Crisis, 1788–9].

Dixon, Campbell, 'Sheridan', in Leonard Russell (ed.), *English Wits* (London: Hutchinson, 1940) pp. 171–96 [considers Sheridan as a man of genius].

[Dowe, W.,] 'The Sheridans – A Rare Literary Family', *National Quarterly Review*, 36 (Jan 1878) 117–34 [describes the literary achievements of the Sheridan family].

Drury, Charles, 'The Linleys of Norton', *A Sheaf of Essays by a Sheffield Antiquary* (Sheffield: J. W. Northend, 1929) pp. 126–9 [the daughters of Thomas Linley, Jr: Helen, Caroline, and Jane Georgina].

Durant, Jack D., *Richard Brinsley Sheridan*, Twayne's English Authors series (Boston, Mass.: G. K. Hall, 1975) [offers a descriptive introductory survey of Sheridan's literary work].

[Earle, William,] *Sheridan and His Times, by an Octogenarian, who Stood by His Knee in Youth and Sat at His Table in Manhood*, 2 vols (London: J. F. Hope, 1859) [contains much gossip and a few characteristic anecdotes].

Fiske, Roger, 'The Linleys 1775–1780', *English Theatre Music in the Eighteenth Century* (London: Oxford University Press, 1973) pp. 431–21 [touches upon Sheridan's professional relationship with the two Thomas Linleys, father and son].

Fitzgerald, Percy, *The Lives of the Sheridans*, 2 vols (London: R. Bentley and Son, 1886) [recounts the many-sided life of Sheridan].

——, 'The Loves of Famous Men, No. VII: Sheridan', *Belgravia*, 14 (Apr 1871) 163–75 [recounts the relationship between Sheridan and Elizabeth Linley].

——, 'The Real Sheridan', *New Century Review*, 1 (May 1897) 395–403; (June 1897) 503–8 [complains that Fraser Rae's biography of Sheridan, approved by Lord Dufferin, shamelessly whitewashes its subject].

——, 'Sheridan and His Wives', *Gentleman's Magazine*, 260 (Jan 1886) 42–61 [shows that both Sheridan's wives were gradually alienated by his selfish and vainglorious infidelities and extravagances till they ended in disliking him].

——, *Sheridan Whitewashed: An Examination of the New Life by Mr Fraser Rae: with an Account of the Linley Letters – Said to Have Been Found in Barrels in Drury Lane* (London: Downey, 1897) [attacks the Marquis of Dufferin and Ava and W. Fraser Rae].

Foss, Kenelm, *Here Lies Richard Brinsley Sheridan* (London: Martin Secker, 1939) [provides a character-study of Sheridan].

George IV, *The Correspondence of George, Prince of Wales*, ed. A. Aspinall, 8 vols (New York: Oxford University Press, 1963–71) [contains several references to Sheridan].

'Gibbs, Walter' [Joseph Walter Cove], *Sheridan* (London: Dent, 1947) [recounts Sheridan's life on the basis of his 'three careers', those of playwright, of theatre manager, and of Member of Parliament.]

——, 'Sheridan against Warren Hastings,' *Quarterly Journal of Speech*, 34 (Dec 1948) 464–8 [recounts the circumstances surrounding Sheridan's great speeches against Hastings].

Gilfallan, George, 'Modern British Orators – No. II: R. B. Sheridan', *Hogg's Instructor*, 3rd ser., 1 (Nov 1853) 361–70 [presents an unfavourable picture of Sheridan as an orator and enumerates his many defects].

Glasgow, Alice, *Sheridan of Drury Lane: A Biography* (New York: Frederick A. Stokes, 1940)

Green, Emanuel, *Richard Brinsley Sheridan and Thomas Linley: Their Residences at Bath, with a Notice of the Sheridan Grotto* (Bath: Herald Office, 1904) [fixes the residential address of the Sheridans in Bath at 9 New King Street].

——, *Sheridan and Mathews at Bath: A Criticism of the Story as Told in the Several Sheridan Biographies* (London: Harrison and Sons, 1912) [provides information about Sheridan's career in Bath].

——, *Thomas Linley, Richard Brinsley Sheridan, and Thomas Mathews: Their Connection with Bath* (Bath: Herald Office, 1903) [includes much material from the files of the *Bath Chronicle*.]

Heron, D. C., 'Sheridan', *The Afternoon Lectures on Literature and Art. Delivered in the Theatre of the Royal College of Science, S. Stephen's Green, Dublin, in the Years 1867 and 1868* (Dublin: W. McGee, 1869) pp. 213–34 [recounts the life of Sheridan and pays homage to him].

Hunt, Leigh, 'Biographical and Critical Sketch', in Hunt (ed.), *The Dramatic Works of Richard Brinsley Sheridan* (London: Edward Moxon, 1840) pp. vii–xv [explains the waste of Sheridan's gifts].

[——], 'The Late Mr Sheridan', *Examiner*, 446 (14 July 1816) 433–6 [sketches the life of Sheridan, and speaks of him as an orator, a wit, a dramatist and a man].

Jefferson, Joseph, *The Autobiography of Joseph Jefferson* (New York: Century, 1889) pp. 397–403 [recollects the staging of Jefferson's own version of *The Rivals*].

'Kelly's Memoirs', [Colburn's] *New Monthly Magazine*, 14 (1825) 487-94 [includes some recollections of Sheridan].

Landfield, Jerome B., 'Man of Action', *Saturday Review*, 36 (21 Feb 1953) 25 [identifies the 'most outstanding single action of Sheridan's parliamentary career as being his decisive conduct in putting down the naval mutinies of 1797].

——, 'Sheridan's Maiden Speech: Indictment by Anecdote', *Quarterly Journal of Speech*, 43 (Apr 1957) 137–42 [examines the tradition that Sheridan's maiden speech in the House of Commons was unsuccessful].

——, 'The Triumph and Failure of Sheridan's Speeches against Hastings', *Speech Monographs*, 28 (Aug 1961) 143–56 [inquires why Sheridan's orations, though they created an immediate sensation, failed to inspire continued admiration].

Mahoney, John L., 'Sheridan on Hastings: The Classical Oration and Eighteenth-Century Politics', *Burke Newsletter*, 6 (1965) 414–22 [demonstrates that Sheridan's Westminster Hall speech against Hastings employed the classical orational pattern].

Marshall, P. J., *The Impeachment of Warren Hastings* (London: Oxford University Press, 1965) [mentions Sheridan's involvement in the impeachment and sets out the issues argued in his speeches against Hastings].

Matthews, Brander, 'Richard Brinsley Sheridan and His Biographers', *Princeton Review*, new ser., 13 (May 1884) 292–303 [surveys the early biographies of Sheridan].

'Memoir of the Right Honourable Richard Brinsley Sheridan', *The Speeches of the Right Honourable Brinsley Sheridan. With a Sketch of His Life. Edited by a Constitutional Friend* [Sir John Phillipart?] (London: Henry G. Bohn, 1842) I, i–xvi.

Montague-Smith, Patrick W., 'Sheridan's Maternal Ancestors, the Chamberlaines of Kingsclere', *Genealogists' Magazine*, 15 (Mar 1967) 319–30 [observes that much of Sheridan's brilliance must have been inherited from his gifted mother, Frances Chamberlaine].

Moore, Thomas, *Memoirs, Journals, and Correspondence*, ed. Lord John Russell, 8 vols (London: Longman, Brown, Green, and Longmans, 1853–6) [includes some anecdotes of Sheridan].

——, *Memoirs of the Life of the Right Honourable Richard Brinsley Sheridan* (London: Longman, Hurst, Rees, Orme, Brown and Green, 1825) [the 5th edn, 2 vols, 1827, contains a new preface making some important corrections].

Morwood, James, *The Life and Works of Richard Brinsley Sheridan* (Edinburgh: Scottish Academic Press, 1985) [provides a reasonably extended biography coupled with a critical discussion of the major plays].

Motley, Mary, *Morning Glory* (London: Longmans, Green, 1961) pp. 272–4 [describes the loss of valuable Sheridan manuscripts in a boating accident].
'Mr Sheridan', *The Times*, 8 July 1816, p. 3 [obituary].
'Mr Sheridan's Funeral', *The Times*, 15 July 1816, p. 3.
'News in Brief', *The Times*, 10 Nov 1954, p. 3 [reports that 'Plaques are to be affixed by London County Council to No. 10, Hertford Street, W., to commemorate the residence there of General John Burgoyne and Richard Brinsley Sheridan'].
Nicoll, Henry James, *Great Orators: Burke, Fox, Sheridan, Pitt* (Edinburgh: Macniven and Wallace; London: Frederick Warne, 1880) pp. 149–204 [surveys Sheridan's literary and political careers].
Norton, Caroline, 'Books of Gossip: Sheridan and His Biographers', *Macmillan's Magazine*, 3 (Jan 1861) 173–9 [the granddaughter of Sheridan attacks 'anecdotical' biographers who slay Sheridan's character].
Oliphant, Margaret, *Sheridan*, English Men of Letters series (London: Macmillan, 1883) [presents Sheridan's life and work].
Oliver, Robert T., *Four Who Spoke Out: Burke, Fox, Sheridan and Pitt* (Syracuse, NY: Syracuse University Press, 1946) [surveys Sheridan's political career].
Patmore, Peter George, 'Richard Brinsley Sheridan and Thomas Sheridan', *My Friends and Acquaintance: Being Memorials, Mind-Portraits and Personal Recollections of Deceased Celebrities of the Nineteenth Century with Selections from their Unpublished Letters* (London: Saunders and Otley, 1854) III, 255–340 [includes anecdotes of Sheridan and his son when he was a boy].
Pearson, Hesketh, 'Richard Brinsley Sheridan', in *Lives of the Wits* (London: Heinemann, 1962) pp. 70–123 [considers Sheridan 'the wittiest and most fascinating character of his age'].
Peterson, Houston (ed.), 'Richard Brinsley Sheridan Brings the Hastings Trial to a Climax', *A Treasury of the World's Great Speeches* (New York: Simon and Schuster, 1954) pp. 180–4 [prints 'the peroration on the fourth day' (13 June 1788)].
'Plaque to Commemorate Sheridan's Elopement', *The Times*, 6 Feb 1955, p. 10 [announces the unveiling at 11 Royal Crescent, Bath, of a plaque bearing the inscription 'Thomas Linley lived here and from this house his daughter Elizabeth eloped with Richard Brinsley Sheridan on the evening of 18th March, 1772'].
Price, Cecil, Introduction to *The Letters of Richard Brinsley Sheridan*, ed. Price (Oxford: Clarendon Press, 1966) I, xiii–xx [the letters 'clearly reveal the nature of the man and are a necessary supplement to his actions, speeches, and plays'].
——, 'Sheridan–Linley Documents', *Theatre Notebook*, 21 (Summer

1967) 165–7 [gives brief descriptive accounts of several documents donated to the British Museum, including a copy of the marriage articles of Sheridan and Elizabeth Linley].

Pritchett, V. S., 'Anglo-Irish', *New Statesman*, 72 (12 Aug 1966) 230 [Sheridan as Anglo-Irish].

Rae, W. Fraser, 'More about Sheridan', *Nineteenth Century*, 43 (Feb 1898) 256–65 [collects letters and other documents].

——, 'Richard Brinsley Sheridan', *Fortnightly Review*, 2nd ser., 8 (new series 2) (1867) 310–32 [judges Sheridan as one who 'wrote, as he lived, for the sake of effect'].

——, *Sheridan: A Biography*, 2 vols (London: Richard Bentley, 1896) [written at the suggestion of Sheridan's great-grandson, the Marquis of Dufferin and Ava].

——, 'Sheridan's Brother', *Temple Bar*, 119 (Mar 1900) 396–415 [provides a biographical account of Charles Francis Sheridan].

——, 'Sheridan's Sisters', *Temple Bar*, 118 (Sep 1899) 45–63 [provides biographical accounts of Sheridan's sisters Alicia and Elizabeth].

——,'Sheridan's Sons', *Temple Bar*, 116 (Mar 1899) 407–26 [provides particulars about Sheridan's two sons Tom and Charles Brinsley].

——, *Wilkes, Sheridan, Fox – the Opposition under George III* (London: W. Isbister, 1874) pp. 141–245 [presents a sympathetic portrait of Sheridan].

Reid, Loren D., 'Sheridan's Speech on Mrs Fitzgerald', *Quarterly Journal of Speech*, 33 (Feb 1947) 15–22 [analyses Sheridan's famous speech in defence of Mrs Fitzherbert, a Roman Catholic whom the Prince of Wales married secretly].

Rhodes, R. Crompton, *Harlequin Sheridan, the Man and the Legends* (Oxford: B. H. Blackwell, 1933) [sets out to show Sheridan 'in the round'].

Sadleir, Michael T. H., *The Political Career of Richard Brinsley Sheridan, Followed by Some Hitherto Unpublished Letters of Mrs Sheridan*, the Stanhope Essay for 1912 (Oxford: B. H. Blackwell, 1912).

Sanders, Lloyd C., *Life of Richard Brinsley Sheridan*, Great Writers series (London: Walter Scott, 1890) [acknowledges that Sheridan the man was certainly a riddle].

'Senex', 'Reminiscences: Richard Brinsley Sheridan', *Blackwood's Edinburgh Magazine*, 20 (July 1826) 25–41; (Aug 1826), 201–14 [finds Moore's memoirs of Sheridan in general to be biased and unconvincing].

Sheldon, Esther K., *Thomas Sheridan of Smock-Alley* (Princeton, NJ: Princeton University Press, 1967) [on Sheridan's father].

'Sheridan', *Temple Bar*, 60 (Dec 1880) 488–503; repr. in *Living Age*, 148 (15 Jan 1881) 131–40 [a biographical sketch].

Sheridan, Clare, *To the Four Winds* (London: André Deutsch, 1957)

p. 304 [refers to the sailing mishap which resulted in the loss at sea of the original manuscripts of *The Critic*, *The Duenna*, and *St Patrick's Day*].

Sheridan, Elizabeth, *Betsy Sheridan's Journal: Letters from Sheridan's Sister, 1784–1786 and 1788–1790*, ed. William LeFanu (London: Eyre and Spottiswoode; New Brunswick, NJ: Rutgers University Press, 1960) [prints seventy-one letters written by Elizabeth to her sister Alicia].

Sheridan, Richard Brinsley, 'To the Editor of *The Times*', *The Times*, 3 Nov 1847, p. 8 [reflects an allegation made by W. Baker, coroner for Middlesex, to the effect that one William Stewart Sheridan, an accused matricide, was the grandson of the celebrated Sheridan]. See reply by W. Baker, 'To the Editor of *The Times*', *The Times*, 2 Dec 1847, p. 6; and 'Veritas', 'Mr Sheridan and Mr Baker', *The Times*, 3 Dec 1847, p. 6.

Sheridan, Wilfred, 'Some Account of the Sheridan Family', *Ancestor* (London), no. 9 (Apr 1904) 1–5 [traces the Sheridan line from its beginnings through to the generation of the playwright's grandchildren].

Sheridaniana; or Anecdotes of the Life of Richard Brinsley Sheridan, His Table Talk and Bon Mots (London: Henry Colburn, 1826) [while some of the stories are apocryphal, this book contains some important extracts from contemporary periodicals].

'Sheridan's Grandchildren', *New York Times*, 23 May 1888, p. 6 [announces the death of Sheridan's grandson, Richard Brinsley].

Sherwin, Oscar, *Uncorking Old Sherry: The Life and Times of Richard Brinsley Sheridan* (New York: Twayne Publishers, 1960) [sets Sheridan's life against a backdrop of his age].

Sichel, Walter, *Sheridan, from New and Original Material; Including a Manuscript Diary by Georgiana, Duchess of Devonshire*, 2 vols (London: Constable, 1909) [provides a comprehensive account of Sheridan's life].

'Sketch of the Life and Character of the Late Right Hon. R. B. Sheridan', *Scots Magazine and Edinburgh Literary Miscellany*, 78 (July 1816) 522–9 [obituary].

Smyth, William, *Memoir of Mr Sheridan* (Leeds: J. Cross, 1840).

Stoker, Matilda, 'Sheridan and Miss Linley', *English Illustrated Magazine*, 8 (Apr 1887) 491–511 [argues that Elizabeth Sheridan's affections for her husband remained strong throughout their marriage, as her letters prove].

Stokes, Hugh, *The Devonshire House Circle* (London: H. Jenkins, 1917) [attributes Sheridan's success with the Duchess of Devonshire and her circle to his quick and amiable wit and to his kinship in spirit with the Duchess].

T., L. J., 'Richard Brinsley Sheridan', *Universal Review*, 3 (1860) 75–

98; repr. in *Living Age*, 64 (31 Mar 1860) 771–85 [recounts the life of Sheridan].

[Thornbury,] 'Old Stories Re-Told: Sheridan's Duels with Captain Mathews', *All the Year Round*, 18 (3 Aug 1867) 128–36; repr. in *Every Saturday*, 4 (24 Aug 1867) 227–33 [recounts the two duel episodes].

'Tom Sheridan', *All the Year Round*, 28 (12 Nov 1881) 232–6 [sketches the life of Sheridan's son].

'200th Anniversary of Sheridan's Birth', *The Times*, 31 Oct 1951, p. 8 [describes a ceremony in which wreaths were placed on Sheridan's grave in Westminster Abbey].

Vachell, Horace Annesley, *Great Chameleon: A Biographical Romance* (London: Hutchinson, 1940) [biography of Sheridan].

Walker, Joan, *Marriage of Harlequin: A Biographical Novel of the Important Years in the Life of Richard Brinsley Sheridan* (Toronto: McClelland and Stewart; London: Jarrolds, 1962) [imagines the thoughts and passions motivating Sheridan's life from 1770 to 1792].

Watkins, John, *Memoirs of the Public and Private Life of the Right Honourable Richard Brinsley Sheridan, with a Particular Account of His Family and Connexions*, 2 vols (London: Henry Colburn, 1817) [the first of Sheridan's biographies].

Welldon, J. E. C., 'Sheridan's School Days', *The Times*, 17 Feb 1934, p. 8 [observes that it is a paradox that Sheridan, who was unhappy and unpromising at Harrow, became an important literary figure].

'Wharton, Grace and Philip' [Katherine Byerley Thomson and John Cockburn Thomson], 'Richard Brinsley Sheridan', *The Wits and Beaux of Society* (London: James Hogg and Sons, 1860) II, 97–161 [provides a scurrilous sketch of Sheridan].

Index

The figures in parentheses after entry numbers indicate the number of references. 'Mc' is treated as if spelt 'Mac'.

Aickin, Frank, 85
Aikenhead, Mr, 6
Angelo, Henry, 21
Archdall, Richard, 2
Aristænetus, xvi, 109(2)

Backbite, Sir Benjamin, 120
Baker, Sir G., 70
Bannister, John (Jack), x, 35, 84(4), 90
Barnett, William, 19–20, 21(n)
Barry, Spranger, 118(2)
Bath, x, xvi, 1, 2(n), 9, 12–15, 18, 19, 23, 25(n), 31, 55, 74, 88, 114, 118(2), 119, 122, 123(2)
Bath Chronicle, xvi, 9(2), 10, 13(n), 14, 15
Battle of Hastings, The (Cumberland), 27, 29(7), 30(3), 31, 33(2)
Bedford Coffee-house, 13
Beefsteak Club, x
Beggar's Opera, The (Gay), 85, 96, 118, 121
Bernard, John, x, xiv(n)
Bessborough, Lady, 51, 53(n), 54, 66–7, 78, 103, 105, 110
Bessborough, Lord, 67(2)
Bingham, Madeleine, 27(n)
Blois, France, xvi, 2(n)
Boaden, James, 33, 35
Boswell, James, xi, 126
Braham, John, 82(3)
Brooks's Club, x, xvii, 58, 74, 101, 110, 111(n)
Brougham, Lord Henry, 92–5, 105, 106–7
Bruton Street, London, 49(n), 84, 88

Bryant, William Cullen, 134–7
Burgess, John, 41, 45
Burke, Edmund, xvii, 39, 40(2), 41, 42(2), 43, 44, 71, 72, 92, 109, 112, 131, 138
Burney, Frances (Fanny), xi, 36
Burnham Grove, 23(n)
Butler, Charles, 128–33
Byron, Lord, x, 96–7, 111–13

Candour, Mrs, 120(2)
Canning, George, 53(n)
Canning, Mrs Stratford, 50–3, 55–7, 62–3
Carlton House, 131
Castle Spectre, The (Lewis), 113(3)
Castle Tavern, 13
Chamberlaine, Richard, xvi, 5, 6, 8, 14, 18(n)
Chatsworth, x
Choleric Man, The, 87
Cholmondeley, Mrs, xi
Clarence, Duke of, 51, 52(3)
Coleridge, Samuel Taylor, 65–6
Collier, Jeremy, 34
Colman, George, x, 28, 33(3), 34(n), 86
Conversations of Lord Byron (Medwin), 112
Covent Garden Theatre, xvi(2), xvii(2), 24, 25(n), 33, 118, 121, 128
Creevey, Thomas, 5(n), 81–2
Creevy Papers, The, 81–2
Crewe, Frances Lady, xi, 36(2), 42, 49, 108(2)
Crewe, Lord, 108(4), 111(n)
Crewe Hall, 49, 50(n), 108

147

148 INDEX

Croker, John Wilson, 97
Crouch, Mrs, 71(2), 85
Crutched Friars, 12
Cumberland, George, 29
Cumberland, Richard, 27–34
Cymon, 83–4, 91(n)

d'Arblay, Madame. *See* Burney, Frances
Davies, Tom, 29, 30, 35
Davy, Sir Humphrey, x
De Genlis, Madame, 61(2), 111(n)
de Retz, Cardinal, 131, 133(n)
Devonshire, Georgiana, Duchess of, x, xiv, 38(n), 53(n), 67(2)
Devonshire House, 38(n)
Dibdin, Charles, 30, 45
Dolman, Dr R., 8(2), 12(n)
Dorset Street, xvi
Douglas, Sir John, 97
Dowton, William, 86(2), 87(5), 90
Dramatic Works of Richard Brinsley Sheridan (Hunt), xiv
Drury Lane Theatre, x, xi, xvii(9), xviii(3), 23(n), 26(2), 29, 31(2), 35, 37, 66, 69, 83, 86, 87, 89(8), 90(3), 91(n), 92, 97, 101, 108, 112(n), 113, 122, 123, 132, 138
Dufferin and Ava, the Marquis of, 137–8
Duncannon, Lady (afterwards Lady Bessborough). *See* Bessborough, Lady
Dundas, Henry, Viscount Melville, 39, 75
Durant, Jack D., viii, xiv

Earle, William, xiii, xiv, 32, 35, 107
Effingham, Countess of, 70
Elliot, Sir Gilbert, 40
Ewart, John, 8, 16, 17(n)
Ewart, Simon, 8, 13, 16, 17(n)

Fitzgerald, Lord Edward, xviii
Fitzgerald, Percy, xiii, xiv, 9(2), 28, 34(n), 37
Fitzwilliam, Lord, 76
Fordyce, Lady Margaret, 114(4), 115

Fox, Charles James, x(4), xii(2), xvii(2), xviii, 38, 39(2), 40, 41, 42, 44, 45, 52, 76, 92, 98, 106, 111, 112, 131, 133, 137, 138
Frith Street, 23(n)
Fugitive, The (Richardson), 108

Garrick, David, xii, xvii(2), 21, 23(n), 25(n), 26, 27(3), 28(5), 29(7), 34(n), 61, 89, 96, 122(3)
Gay, John, 121
Geary, Sir William, 130
George III, 70, 77(4), 128
George IV, xviii(3), 52, 70, 74(5), 79(4), 80(2), 81, 82, 83(5), 104(3), 105(n), 107, 136
Goldsmidt, Abraham, 82, 83
Goldsmith, Oliver, 34
Good-natured Man, The (Goldsmith), 87
Goodricke, Sir John, 126
Gower, Lord Granville Leveson, 66–8
Green, Emanuel, 13(n)
Grey, Lord Charles, 75, 76, 97

Halhed, Nathaniel, 2, 109
Hare, James, x, 18(n), 38, 68, 75(4)
Harlequin Sheridan (Rhodes), 9(2)
Hastings, Warren, xvii(3), 41(3), 42(2), 43, 45, 69, 70, 81(4), 82(n), 93, 108
Haymarket Theatre, 34(n), 91(n)
Hazlitt, William, ix
Hercules Pillars, 12, 13
Historical Sketches (Brougham), 92–5
Holland, Elizabeth, Lady, xi, 73–7
Holland, Lord Henry, xi, 4(n), 74, 75(4), 76(2), 78(n), 83, 96, 106(n), 110
Honey Moon, The, 87(2)
Hunt, Leigh, xiii, xiv, 35

Inchbald, Elizabeth, 121
Ireland, W. H., 35
Iron Chest, The (Colman), 64(n)

INDEX

Jarvis, Dr Daniel, 46
Jerningham, Edward, 132(2)
Johnson, Jack, 87
Johnson, Dr Samuel, xvii, 23(n), 26(n), 46(n), 112(n), 121(2), 126, 132
Jones, Sir William, 4
Journal of Elizabeth Lady Holland, The, 73–7

Kelly, Michael, xi, 83–91, 129
Kemble, John Philip, 69, 71(3), 72(2), 73(n), 83, 84
King, Thomas, 69
Kingsdown, nr Bath, 15, 19, 54
Knight, Captain, 12, 13(2)

Lansdown, Lord, 73(2), 74(2)
Lee, Sophia, 123
Lefanu, Alicia (Sheridan's niece), 5, 7(n), 114
Lefanu, Henry, 9(n), 49(n)
Lefanu, Joseph, 2(n), 49
Leigh, Mr and Mrs, 56, 57(n)
Letters and Journals (Byron), 111
Lewis, Matthew Gregory, 112, 113(5)
Life and Correspondence of Charles Mathews, 82–3
Life and Times (Reynolds), 25
Life of Byron (Moore), 96
Life of Richard Brinsley Sheridan (Sanders), xiv, 24
Lincoln's Inn Fields, 89(2)
Lindsay, Anne Lady, 114
Linley, Elizabeth. *See* Sheridan, Elizabeth (wife)
Linley, Jane (later Mrs Charles Ward), 123
Linley, Maria, 118, 122(2), 123
Linley, Mary, née Johnson (Mrs Thomas Linley), 21, 56
Linley, Mary (later Mrs Richard Tickell), 8, 9(n), 11, 12(n), 23, 111(n), 118, 123(2)
Linley, Revd Ozias, 123
Linley, Samuel, 122
Linley, Thomas, 7, 9(2), 12(n), 24, 25(n), 87, 88

Linley, Thomas, Jr (Tom), 7, 24, 25(n), 87, 88, 118, 122(3)
Linley, William, 123
Literary Club, xi, xvii, 121
Lives of the Sheridans, The (Fitzgerald), xiv, 9, 28, 34(n)
Long, Walter, 7, 9(n)

Macbeth (Shakespeare), 38(n)
MacMahon, Colonel Sir John, 99(4), 100(9), 101(3), 102(2), 103(3), 104(3)
Margate, 47, 48
Marylebone Church, London, xvi
Mathews, Anne, 82–3
Mathews, Charles, 34(3), 35, 82–3
Mathews, Thomas, xvi(3), 2(n), 7, 9(2), 10, 11, 12–20, 21(n), 54(n)
Medwin, Thomas, 112
Memoir of Mr Sheridan (Smyth), xiv, 57
Memoirs, Journals, and Correspondence (Moore), 18(n)
Memoirs of the Life and Writings of Mrs Frances Sheridan, 5
Memoirs of the Life of . . . Sheridan (Moore), xiv, 2, 11, 16, 23, 42, 46, 55, 62, 107(n), 128
Memoirs of the Public and Private Life of . . . Sheridan (Watkins), xiv, 31, 32, 35(2), 114
Middle Temple, xvi, 117
Milton, John, 4
Moira, Lord, 98, 99(5), 104
Moore, Peter, 106(n), 107(n)
Moore, Thomas, ix, xii, xiii(2), xiv(n), 2, 11, 16, 18(n), 42, 46, 55, 62, 93, 95, 96, 106, 107(n), 109, 112(n), 113, 128, 135, 138
Morris, Edward, 57, 58(3), 59(4), 60(3), 61(5)

Note of Hand, The (Cumberland), 31

Ogle, Hester Jane. *See* Sheridan, Hester (second wife)
Ogle, Newton, xviii, 110

Ogle, Sukey, ix
Oliphant, Margaret, xiii(2), xiv, 38
Opera House, 85, 86, 89, 90, 91(n)
Orchard Street, London, xvi, 21, 23(n), 118
Osorio (Coleridge), 66(n)
Ossory, Countess of, 41

Parade Coffee-house, Bath, 13(n)
Parr, Dr Samuel, 2–4, 5, 58, 88
Paumier, Captain, 19(3), 20(5)
Pavilion, The, 87
Perceval, Spencer, 133
Piazza Coffee-house, 83
Pitt, William, xii, 39, 40, 41, 42, 44, 45, 70(4), 72, 92, 94, 138
Plagiary, Sir Fretful, 32(5), 33(9), 34(3), 35(2)
Purdon, Mrs, 6

Rae, W. Fraser, xiii, xiv, 1, 7, 12, 13, 17, 26, 43, 49, 95, 105(n), 137
Recollections of a Long Life (Broughton), 105, 106
Recollections of the Table-Talk of Samuel Rogers, 108–10
Reminiscences (Angelo), 21
Reminiscences (Butler), 128–33
Reminiscences of Michael Kelly, 83–91
Remorse (Coleridge), 65–6
Retrospections of the Stage (Bernard), xiv
Reynolds, Frederic, 25
Reynolds, Sir Joshua, xvii
Rhodes, R. Compton, 9(2)
Richard Brinsley Sheridan: A Reference Guide (Durant), xiv
Richardson, Joseph, 58(4), 59(4), 72(4), 73(n), 78, 108(4), 111(n)
Rogers, Samuel, x, 108–10
Royal Crescent, Bath, 9(n)

Sanders, Lloyd C., xiii, xiv, 24
Savage, Richard, 111, 112(n), 132
Savile Row, xviii, 100, 106(n)
Scott, Sir Walter, 34(2), 35(2), 110
Sheridan, Alicia (sister) [Mrs Joseph Lefanu], xvi, 1, 2(n), 7, 43(n), 44(n), 48, 49(n), 56, 57(n), 63(n)

Sheridan, Charles Brinsley (second son), xviii(2)
Sheridan, Charles Francis (brother), xvi, xviii, 1, 2(n), 11, 12(n), 13, 14, 16, 17(n), 18, 23(n), 27(n), 47, 79–81, 106, 125, 126(6)
Sheridan, Elizabeth [Eliza] (first wife), ix, xvi(2), xviii, 2(n), 7, 9(n), 11, 12(n), 14, 23, 25(n), 36, 43, 46, 48, 49, 50, 54, 55–7, 115, 116(2), 117, 118(2), 122, 124, 131, 136
Sheridan, Elizabeth [Betsy] (sister) [Mrs Henry Lefanu], xvi, 1, 2(n), 7, 9(n), 42, 43, 46, 48, 119(2), 123, 124, 128(n)
Sheridan, Frances Anne (mother), xvi, 1, 2(n), 5, 23(n), 128(n)
Sheridan, Hester [Esther] (second wife), xii, xviii(2), 64(2), 78(n), 100, 103, 104, 105(n), 112(n), 131
Sheridan, Mary (infant daughter), xviii, 56, 57(n), 62–3, 125(2), 128(n)
Sheridan, Richard Brinsley, born, xvi; christened, xvi; attends Samuel Whyte's grammar school, xvi, 2(n); attends Harrow School, xvi, 1, 2–4, 5–7; studies law, xvi; elopes, xvi, 7–9, 10; fights duels, xvi, 1, 2(n), 12–20, 119; marries, xvi, 23(n); in Dublin, 1, 2(n); in Bath, xvi, 6, 8(n), 9(n), 12, 13(n), 14, 15, 19–20, 56; in London, xvi, 8, 12–14, 21ff.; in Margate, 47, 48, 49; at Wanstead, 60, 61, 64, 125; at Isleworth, 56, 58–61, 125(3); in Deepdene, 49; in Lille, 8(2), 12(n); in Dunkirk, 8(3), 9(2); in Calais, 8; in France, xvi, 1, 2, 8, 10, 12, 13(n); his appearance, 1, 36, 61; his countenance, 1, 3, 36, 39, 42, 113; his eyes, 1, 3, 61, 110, 113; his forehead, 113; his voice, 39, 40, 42, 94; his intellect, 3; his wit, x(2), 1, 38, 39, 44, 74, 93, 112(n), 113, 129, 135, 138; his satire, 39, 113; his tact, 39; his charm, xi; his conviviality, 138; his pride, 107; his

INDEX

Sheridan, Richard Brinsley—*continued*
conversation, ix, x(2), xi(2), 110;
his contradictory character, ix, xiii,
113, 134–6, 137; his silence, xi, 110;
his superstition, 88, 130; his pranks,
3, 108; his love of pleasure, 134,
135, 136; his indolence, 134, 135,
136; his intemperate habits, 95; his
drinking, 49, 78, 102, 110, 111, 138;
his love of extravagance, xiii, 6; his
unpunctuality, xiii, 58, 59–61,
66(n), 73, 86, 98, 99, 132, 134; his
infidelities, ix, 50(n), 51, 52, 66–8,
136; his pecuniary troubles, ix,
xviii(2), 5, 63–4, 85, 95, 101, 102,
103, 111, 117, 130, 131, 133, 137,
138; in Parliament, xvii, xviii(4),
39–41, 42, 43, 44, 73, 81, 90, 92,
98, 99, 101, 128, 133, 134, 135; as
a politician, xi, xii, xvii, xviii,
38(n), 40(n), 70, 74, 92, 93, 95, 97,
126, 130, 134, 137; as an orator,
xii, 5, 40, 41, 42, 44, 92, 93, 108,
132; as a theatre manager, xi, xvii,
xviii, 27(2), 33, 37, 38(n), 66(n),
69, 91, 118, 128, 132, 134; as a
dramatist, xi; as a poet, 3, 4, 4(n),
129(2); as a correspondent, ix; and
religion, 110, 111(n), 130, 131;
compared with Aristophanes, 32;
with Pitt, 40, 41, 138; with Burke,
40, 41, 138; with Fox, 40, 41, 138;
his biographers, ix, xii; biographies
of, xii, xiii, 139–46; his illness, 102,
103, 104, 110; his death, xviii, 103,
105; his funeral, 106, 107(n); his
burial, xii, xviii, 106

His Writings
Camp, The, xvii
Critic, The, xi, xvii, 32(4), 33(3), 34,
35, 96
Duenna, The, xvii, 24–5, 96, 118(2),
121, 128, 133, 135
Love Epistles of Aristænetus, The, xvi
Pizarro, xviii, 76(2), 111(7), 112,
113(2)
Rivals, The, x, xi, xvi(2), 23–4, 38,
109, 118, 119, 121, 135

Robinson Crusoe, xvii
St Patrick's Day, xvii
School for Scandal, The, ix, xi, xvii,
25–6, 31(3), 32, 50(n), 72, 96,
109, 118, 119(5), 120(2), 121,
128(n), 129, 133, 135
Trip to Scarborough, A, xvii
Sheridan, Thomas (father), xii, xvi,
xvii, 1, 3(2), 4(2), 5, 7(n), 17–18,
23(n), 26, 46–7, 73(n), 118
Sheridan, Revd Dr Thomas
(grandfather), 5(n), 116
Sheridan, Thomas [Tom] (son), xiii,
xvii, xviii(2), 53(n), 55, 56(3), 57,
61, 63(n), 79, 88, 125(2)
Sheridan, William (great-
grandfather), 116
Sheridan (Oliphant), xiv, 38
Sheridan: A Biography (Rae), xiv, 1,
7–8, 12–14, 17–18, 26, 43, 49,
105(n), 137–8
Sheridan and His Times (Earle), xiv, 35,
107
Sheridan and Mathews at Bath (Green),
13(n)
Sheridan, from New and Original Material
(Sichel), xiv, 35, 54, 78
Sheridan: The Track of a Comet
(Bingham), 27(n)
Sheridaniana, xiv, 31, 35
Sichel, Walter, xiii, xiv, 35, 54, 78
Siddons, Sarah, 37–8
Smith, Sir Sydney, 98
Smyth, William, xiii, xiv, 57–61,
63–4, 125
Sneer, 33, 34
Sneerwell, Lady, 120
Staël, Madame de, x
Stafford, 40(n), 98(2), 132(3)
Storace, Stephen, 83, 84
Sumner, Dr Robert, 1, 3(6), 4, 5, 7
Surface, Charles, 119
Surface, Sir Oliver, ix
Swift, Jonathan, 4

Taylor, A., 45
Teazle, Lady, 34, 120
Teazle, Sir Peter, ix

Temple Bar, 79, 80
Thanet, Lord, 18
Tickell, Betty, 55, 56, 88
Tickell, Mary, 53(n)
Tickell, Richard, 47, 108(4), 111(n), 123(2)
Tierney, George, 73, 74(5), 75, 76(3)
Times, The (London), 9(n)
Townshend, Charles, x, 38
Townshend, Lord John, x, 18(n), 38, 76, 108(2)

Vaughan, Hat, 102, 103(3), 104(4)
Vortigern, (Ireland), 35

Wade, Captain William, 19
Walpole, Sir Horace, 41, 42(n)
Waltham Abbey, xvi

Watkins, John, xii, xiv(n), 31, 32, 35(2), 114–27
Westminster Abbey, xviii, 106
Westminster Hall, xvii, 42, 43(n), 69, 70, 81, 93, 108
Whig Party, xi, xvii, 111, 112, 137
Whitbread, Samuel, x, 97(6), 98(3), 101(2), 103(2)
White, Lydia, 110, 111(n)
Whyte, Samuel, xvi, 2(n)
Wilkes, John, 88
Williams, Stanley Thomas, 27
Wilson, Richard, 89
Windham, William, xi
Windsor, 5
Woodfall, William, 92, 95(n)
Wraxall, Sir Nathaniel, 39–40
Wyatt, James, 21

York, Duke of, 107(n), 109

OHIO UNIVERSITY LIBRARY